The Designer's Guide to Disk Drives

Contents

Introduction

There are perhaps as many ways to write a book as there are reasons for writing it. The purpose of this introduction, therefore, is to make clear both my reasons for writing about disk drives and my method of doing so. I want you to understand the way I view the material that you'll be reading. Because your time is important, before you invest a great deal of time reading a book, you should get an idea of whether it will be stuffy or friendly, useful or ordinary. In short, you need to know if it's your kind of book.

This book is intended to be a straightforward guide, as its name implies. There's little here that is truly original in the sense that a novel is original. The information itself comes from the disk vendors and OEM (original equipment manufacturer) engineers who pass along the news and details of their successes and failures to me. I have attempted to distill this data into a concise package that makes the large body of knowledge available from these sources more easily digestible. It is quite easy to get overwhelmed by too much data. My attempt is to point you to the most useful and the most applicable information, and tell you why it is important.

This book focuses on two major themes: the theory of the disk as an important computer system component (the microcosmic view) and a look at the disk as a complete peripheral in its own right (the macrocosmic view). The two perspectives, taken together, represent a complete picture. The two views combine the information a designer needs to design a disk with the information a system integrator needs to put it into an effective package.

MICROCOSMIC DISK

The ostensible purpose of adding a disk drive, any disk drive, to a computer system is to improve its performance—that is, to equip it to do a particular job. This idea hinges on the assumption that the drive will somehow furnish the host processor with storage space far in excess of what it can directly address or support. And, properly integrated into the system, a disk does precisely that. But at a price. A price which includes more than just the money you pay for the disk drive hardware. This book is dedicated to helping you understand the full price you are about to pay for a disk, regardless of the disk drive you ultimately select.

Successfully building a useful computer system requires that you understand the components that go into it. You must take firm hold of the advantages and limitations that a particular component design offers. Every designer knows this simple fact, yet the effort of coming to understand the bits and pieces of a design is often neglected.

In the shuffle of putting together something that works—that is, something that meets the basic system specifications and cost considerations—there's little time for in-depth analysis. Yet this analysis can prove crucial to the system's long-term performance. Unlike the simple-minded information you get from a data sheet, application note, or even a design article, this analysis positions the component, showing its requirements as well as its contributions to the total system integration effort.

A technical magazine, such as *EDN,* where I've had the good fortune of being the Western Editor covering computers and peripherals for the last few years, enjoys the luxury of being able to view each new technology—its uses and impacts on design—in remarkable depth and with some leisure. The emphasis is on the application of technology, rather than reporting the latest news. There's an opportunity to take a long, hard look at the device itself—the microcosmic disk. There's time to ask if the advantages are truly worth the price.

A book, free of the page constraints imposed by paid advertising and the enormous costs of mailing, has this advantage to an even greater extent. This book in particular allows me the unusual and enviable opportunity of taking an unhurried look at disk technology itself and the means of putting it to work. Once these first two points become part of our decision framework, there's still time to examine the way you should specify disk products.

Disk drives, both hard disks and floppy disks, thrive in an extremely competitive environment. Thus, their design, packaging, and specifications change rapidly. Available models offer a rich and diverse selection of performance, cost, size, ease of use, and capacity trade-offs. Weighing these choices and choosing the optimum drive is an important aspect of your job, not one to be passed on to the purchasing department lightly. The right choice can lead to a system that customers find cost-effective and efficient. The wrong choice often results in a chaotic system unable to meet the needs of its users.

MACROCOSMIC DISK

Learning to use any electronic component effectively directly involves two of your most important senses: the sense of wonder and of discovery. A well-developed sense of discovery will lead you to an understanding of the exact nature of the component—not only how it functions, but also the range of capabilities that its manufacturer designed into it. This study reveals the essential microcosmic disk that we've discussed.

A properly functioning sense of wonder, however, provides a larger picture. You guessed it—a picture of the macrocosmic role the disk has in the overall system operation. It motivates you to explore application possibilities that even the component's manufacturer might not have thought of. Innovators, before they can innovate, must first abandon any idea that the ways already traveled are the best, or only, ways to travel.

Combining these two senses (or sensibilities) with solid design strategies—good engineering practices—should therefore give you a clear vision of the best possible use of the best possible part in your system application. Although this bromide holds true for even the simplest system component, such as a resistor, it becomes especially relevant and important when you are considering an extremely sophisticated and complex system component such as a disk drive.

The effectiveness of the disk, after all, has repercussions throughout the rest of the system. An improperly chosen disk can lead to I/O bottlenecks, insufficient storage capacity for the application, or other fatal inefficiencies.

Picking the proper component and applying it intelligently in the system you are building requires that you take some extra time to really understand the system itself. The best-performing component might not be the most suitable component. The most costly disk might not be the best-performing product for your application.

The appropriate concept to keep in mind is that of cost-effectiveness. You'll find that you don't always get what you pay for when casting about for peripherals. And price, availability, and vendor support can prove mighty factors in an intelligent purchasing decision. A part that is priced low but unavailable for weeks or months might cost you far more than one that has a higher price but is available off the shelf.

One of the tricks to properly specifying disks involves learning to accurately weigh the relative advantages and disadvantages of various drive technologies. The value of the solutions each manufacturer adopts in solving the technical problems of storing information on a disk are not all equal.

To help unravel this specification and estimation, we will develop some guidelines that you should consider as little more than starting points for your analysis. Although we will address many of the trade-offs explicitly, new technologies—new solutions—will demand that you rethink the issues. Some of our guidelines will withstand the onslaughts of fundamental technological change, but many will not.

As optical disks become more pervasive, for example, the price/performance trade-offs between optical disks and magnetic media will swing wildly. And certainly optical disks will not be the last challenge to the dominance of the current crop of rotating media. But the exercise of developing guidelines is far from futile since it will take us through the process of evaluating a new technology—a process you can repeat for whatever changes come along next.

GETTING ALONG WITH OTHERS

Besides evaluating the pluses and minuses of particular technologies, this book will consider the impact of industry standards on your design and product selection—standards in the media, drive mechanics, and electronic interfaces. The desire to establish standards has led many manufacturers to abandon designs they prefer for designs other manufacturers will accept. The ultimate system design goal, after all, is to produce not just a good system, but a marketable system. And *industry standard* remains, fortunately or unfortunately, a highly touted term in marketing circles.

Reading this book should leave you with a warm feeling about disks and a clear idea of how to use them. They can define, to a large degree, the system's ability to fulfill its application tasks. To the extent that the book succeeds, much praise properly belongs to the many disk vendors who furnished information and illustrations. Equally important contributions were made by Carey Hillhouse, who did much of the proofreading and, as always, made many useful suggestions, and the crew at Reston Publishing, who are always supportive, even when manuscripts miss their allotted deadlines. Additional thanks go to Jack Hemenway, who insists that all technical articles don't have to be Chinese food, and Bob Peterson, who used to change Jack's words.

The Designer's Guide to Disk Drives

THE TECHNOLOGY OF DISKS I

1 The Magnetics

The fine art of understanding how best to use the disk for information storage begins with an understanding of how the information is stored on a magnetic disk—how the disk remembers the things it remembers. Many of the advantages and limitations of the various drives which you'll encounter later on will relate directly to the design choices that the disk manufacturer made in working with this so very basic part of the technology.

Each vendor's solution to the problem of storing information has its own strengths and weaknesses; the success or failure of the firm's product in meeting the demands of your application will rest on these factors. But, before we begin examining distinctions, let's look at what they all have in common—their basic method of storing data. All disk drives, other than the new optical disks, rely on the same basic principles. The most popular magic by which a computer stores its information on a rotating disk drive is largely the same as that which provides storage on the linear media of tape recorders, whether cassette or reel-to-reel—magnetic recording.

A SHORT RECORDED HISTORY

The basic technique used today to store data on the media was first demonstrated by a Danish electronic engineer, Valdemar Poulson (also the inventor of the arc generator for radios), at the Paris Exposition of 1900. His idea was based on the principle of induction developed by Michael Faraday in 1831.

Faraday's experiments had shown that changing the magnetic field through a coil (the change of flux) induced a voltage (an electromotive force, or emf) in the coil whose value depended on the time rate of change of the magnetic field. Faraday's law stated that the induced voltage was proportional to the rate of change of flux. An important characteristic of the induced charge is that it is always polarized to oppose the change in the magnetic field.

In an 1888 article in *The Electrical World,* author Oberlin Smith discussed the possibility of storing information through the inductive control of magnetized particles. But it was just an idea. Poulson was the first to actually put the idea to work. He designed and built a device that stored the sounds of a person speaking on a magnetic steel wire.

Poulson's wire recorder ran a steel piano wire past an electromagnet whose field strength was influenced by the amplitude and frequency of the speaker's voice. The frequency of the speech directly affected the rate of field strength changes, and the amplitude of the speech affected the magnitude of the magnet's field. Poulson reversed Faraday's law. The voltage in the magnet's coil produced a magnetic field proportional to the speech and, in turn, stored a magnetic field in the wire. When the wire passed the magnet the next time, the stored field would induce a voltage in the coil. When the voltage was applied to a speaker, the original speech was recreated. It seemed like magic.

This magnetized piano wire thus became the first recording medium. As a storage medium for human speech, it offered many benefits: It was flexible, relatively easy to store, and cheap to produce. Unfortunately, the market wasn't ready. Poulson's company managed to develop only one product before it ran out of money—there was little enthusiasm for an 84–ips (inch/sec) recorder that could store 30 minutes of speech. The device was certainly ahead of its time, but it wasn't of much commercial value. Some major improvements were needed to make it useful beyond its novelty value. Higher recording density and better fidelity would both contribute to the eventual acceptance of magnetic recording devices.

IMPROVING THE MEDIA

The move from wire to today's magnetic media materials—a media made of nonmagnetic substance and then coated with a magnetic material—began in 1927 when J. A. O'Neill received the first U.S. patent for magnetic tape. He dried a liquid containing magnetic particles on a strip of paper. The particles formed a magnetic coating that could retain induced magnetic fields in much the same way that Poulson's wire did.

Today's magnetic tapes are typically based on some sort of plastic film, rather than paper. Plastic provides greater strength and dimensional stability (resistance to stretching, primarily) than most other materials, especially paper. Paper tapes tend to tear easily. You can't count on being able to splice a data tape back together successfully. Thus, plastic quickly proved an attractive alternative to paper.

The magnetic particles that will coat the base material are most often the red form of iron oxide (Fe_2O_3). This is a practical, rather than an optimum, choice. Red iron oxide isn't the best possible material you could find in terms of its magnetic properties. In fact, replacing some of the iron oxide with cobalt helps the coating retain the information stored on it for longer periods of time; coatings of chromium dioxide (CrO_2) offer a larger magnetization level than iron oxides. That is, they store the information as a much larger signal—and, therefore, retain more of the signal's strength and provide a greater immunity to noise. But these alternative materials are also more expensive to produce, too much so to be in common usage. Thus, only those tape or disk drives that actually require higher performance use the more exotic particles.

GETTING INFORMATION ON THE MEDIA

The process of encoding the information from the computer onto the magnetic media involves changing a voltage (logic) level into a magnetization level. This is a little bit different than the recording techniques used to record music or speech on tape, but not much. To record a computer's digital information, the recorder must record one of two logic states: a 1 or a 0. When the information consists solely of these discrete data bits, the data is said to be *discontinuous*. To record music or other analog information, the recorder must accurately record all level variations. The information includes the smallest nuances. This data is *continuous*.

For digital data storage, because there are only two possible logic levels, the media is usually magnetized to its saturation point—magnetized as much as it possibly can be. For this reason this recording technique is called *saturation recording*. By picking the saturation point as the magnetization level, you ensure that you store the largest possible signal. This provides the best signal-to-noise ratio.

To understand what is going on in saturation recording, it's important to remember that solid magnetic materials, such as iron, cobalt, nickel, gadolium, manganese and chromium, contain tiny areas (thousands of atoms thick) that act like independent magnets. These areas are called *domains*. Normally, the domains are scattered randomly throughout the material. The magnetic forces of the various domains cancel each other out, and the material has no net magnetic force. The material is considered demagnetized.

When you bring a magnetic field, the kind produced by a disk's write head, close to the magnetic material, the domains align their boundaries along the lines of the applied force. They now have a net charge that is proportional to the strength of the magnet's field. When you move the magnet away, some of the domains lose their directionality, but others remain aligned. The more domains that remain aligned, the higher the degree of the magnetic charge. It's nearly impossible to keep any domains from losing their directionality but, up to a point, a stronger magnetic field will cause more domains to retain their alignment. The point at which increasing the field doesn't gain you anything is the saturation level.

The actual level of recording—the amount of magnetization that becomes the media's saturation level—is a function of the magnetic characteristics of the media (e.g., the actual magnetic material used, its thickness) as well as the design and physical location of the write head (i.e., its distance from the media during recording).

Writing digital data requires three major components. These components make up the *write channel*. The first component, a current-mode switch, controls the polarity of the current applied to the transducer—the write head. The faster the switch can change polarity, the higher the data rate the write channel can handle. The next component is the write head. Available in many forms, its physical and electrical characteristics will make or break the drive. The last component is the magnetic media. All magnetic media work is the same way, but later you'll see how various media types bring different capabilities to the drive. Whenever you consider the performance of a digital recorder of any kind, you'll have to remember that all three components of the write channel have an impact on that performance. And sometimes upgrading only one won't be enough to gain the desired performance increase.

THE DATA FORMAT

One reasonable way to understand the nature of disks is to think of the disk surface (the media) as just another arrangement of magnetic tape. Both tape and disk drives have three major components, or building blocks: the media, the physical substance which retains the recorded information; the transport, which positions the media; and the read/write channels, the transducers which magnetically transfer the information to and from the magnetic media.

Floppy disks are in fact made of the same material as magnetic tape. Instead of a single strip of the recording media passing under the heads, however, a single disk surface provides several strips arranged such that they take parallel circular paths, forming concentric storage rings, or tracks, as shown in Figure 1–1.

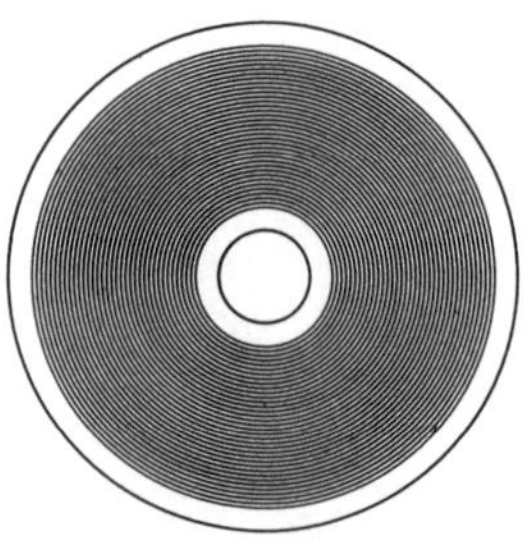

FIGURE 1–1 Data on a disk is arranged in concentric circles termed *tracks*.

The amount of information a disk drive can store on these tracks, and the specific techniques used to put it there, vary widely. But they all (with the notable exception of optical disks) rely on the same basic magnetic-recording techniques used by an everyday home tape recorder.

In a magnetic tape drive the read/write head assembly typically contains a separate read/write head for each track that is physically recorded on the tape's surface, with the head permanently positioned over the track. Regardless of the number of tracks (usually 9, but seldom more than 18), therefore, the tape drive can read any particular track without moving. But disk drives don't usually use multiple read/write heads on a single disk surface. Multiple heads in a disk drive usually indicate that it is using more than one disk surface. Because the head is no longer permanently positioned over the track, the disk drive must incorporate a mechanism to position the head over the particular track that the computer requests the drive to store data in or retrieve data from. The effectiveness of the head-positioning mechanism, therefore, plays a large role in determining the disk's overall performance. And, as you'll see later on, there are a number of competing methods for positioning the heads.

DESIGNING A HEAD

Heads, like most transducers, are designed for a specific task. Thus, the design of the drive's heads will prove a significant factor in establishing the drive's ability to store and retrieve data. High-performance heads will allow the drive's designer to plan on placing more data in any given amount of space on the media. To understand this better, let's look at the way the head operates—the way in which it reads and writes data.

A typical ferrite write head is actually a toroidal structure with a magnetic core and an air gap that looks something like the sketch of an inductive recording head shown in Figure 1–2.

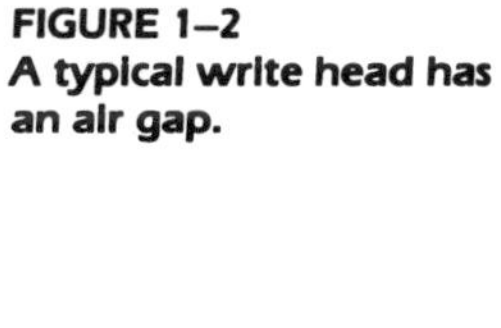

FIGURE 1–2
A typical write head has an air gap.

An electrical pulse sent through the write head's coil induces a magnetic field in its core that transfers to the media. As the media moves past the head, changes in the electrical current through the head's coil (the reversals of the current switch) are recorded in the media.

Take a look at the ferrite head's gap. The gap of a head of this type has two physical dimensions: length and width. The gap width determines how close tracks can be placed together. The narrower the gap width, the more concentric tracks a disk—any sized disk—can have. The relationship is simple. To calculate the maximum number of tracks (the maximum radial density) you can put on the disk's surface (the maximum tpi—tracks per inch) use the equation

$$\text{tpi} = (\text{outer radius} - \text{inner radius})/\text{track width}$$

But you won't want to store data at the maximum possible track density. Such a scheme wouldn't be reliable. There's too much possibility of making errors with the data tracks touching. In a rigid disk that records at 960 tpi, for example, each inch of surface area available will contain no more or less than 960 tracks; therefore, the track centers can't be any closer than 1/960, or 1041.66 μin. to each other. On a 96-tpi floppy diskette, however, track centers are 10416.6 μin. apart.

The gap must be narrower than these track-center distances imply. One track can't run right into the next. There has to be some space between tracks. This space is termed a *guard band.* A 960-tpi disk, for example, requires a head that can write tracks no more than 800 μin. wide. This leaves only 241 μin. between tracks, as you can see from the layout shown in Figure 1–3. This almost seems wasteful when you consider that an 800-μin. track width would allow a maximum of 1250 tpi instead of 960 tpi.

The same inverse relationship of size to recording density applies to the head's gap length, but this time you are changing the linear density rather than the track density. The shorter the gap length, the more flux reversals you can place in a linear inch of disk space. This measurement of linear, or bit, density is called out as either flux reversals per inch (frpi) or, more commonly, flux changes per inch (fci).

FIGURE 1–3
Tracks are separated by blank spaces, termed *guard bands,* which help maintain data integrity.

To find the disk's total storage capacity, you can use the equation

$$\text{capacity} = (\text{fci}) \times (\text{inner track length}) \times (\text{number of tracks})$$

But you have to be careful about simply squeezing data into as tight a package as possible. If you've thought about the geometric shape of the disk, you'll have realized that the inner tracks are shorter than the outer ones. The inner track length, therefore, has to have a higher bit density than the outer tracks in order to store the same amount of data on each track.

It's time to clear up a misconception that might easily arise at this point. This simple discussion has made it sound as if it would be foolish not to use heads with the narrowest possible gap width and length in order to store as much information on the disk as possible. While that is certainly true to some extent, narrowing the gap's dimensions too much can also cause problems. Heads with narrow gaps are harder to manufacture reliably and consistently. There's less margin for error.

And there are mechanical problems. The shorter the gap, the closer the head must fly to the disk surface to ensure that the recording level on the media comes up to the full saturation level. Thus, the aerodynamic design becomes increasingly important. And, the closer together the tracks are, the more critical the head-positioning mechanism. Head-positioning accuracy becomes a limiting factor. Closely related to this idea is the mechanical consideration of nonrepetitive spindle-motor runout. This is the wobble of the spindle as it turns. The closer together the tracks are, the less wobbling of the spindle the drive can tolerate.

Styles to Choose from

The heads in floppy disks come in physical contact with the media when they are reading or writing data. When they touch the media, they are said to be *loaded*. When they aren't touching the media, they are said to be *unloaded*. Figure 1–4 illustrates a typical double-sided head in its loaded position. The top and bottom heads you see in this figure are electrically the same. They are different physically, however, to

FIGURE 1–4
A double-sided floppy head assembly that uses a larger head on the bottom proves simple to manufacture.

Courtesy of Tandon Corp.

ensure that they both load smoothly and without damaging the media.

A newer head design, called the Gumball head, uses two identical heads with rounded sides, as shown in Figure 1–5. This approach, developed by Drivetec, offsets the heads slightly to prevent head bounce. It offers the advantage of having to stock only one head design and one part.

In a single-sided drive you only need one head assembly. The diskette gets sandwiched in between a head and a fixed felt pad. The head presses on the felt pad through the

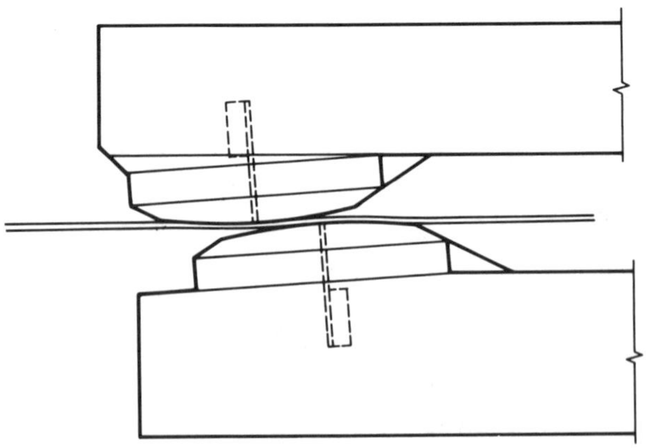

FIGURE 1–5
A Gumball head assembly offsets identical heads with rounded corners.

Courtesy of Drivetec.

Courtesy of Shugart Corp.

FIGURE 1–6
A sealed head-disk assembly helps keep contaminants off of the disk.

diskette. The soft felt absorbs the shock of the head loading and dampens out any bounce that might occur.

One head technology that tries to optimize its design to provide the most storage in the least space is the Winchester head. Winchester heads are intended to be used in sealed assemblies, called head/disk assemblies, or HDAs, such as the one shown in Figure 1–6. These assemblies are important to the successful operation of the disk because they are designed to be almost completely free from contaminants. This cleanliness is especially important in a Winchester drive, more so than in conventional disk drives.

Winchester heads were designed to operate closer to the disk's surface than conventional rigid disk heads, thus allowing designers to take advantage of narrower head gaps and higher linear recording densities. And the techniques they use to get the head close safely have as much to do with aerodynamics as electronics. The Winchester head takes the shape of a platform, called a *slider*. A slider, such as the one shown in Figure 1–7, is just a head assembly, but it is designed as an aerodynamic foil. The air pressure generated by the spinning disk is enough to make it take flight. Because the Winchester head is held off of the disk's surface by an air cushion, or air bearing, you don't have to worry

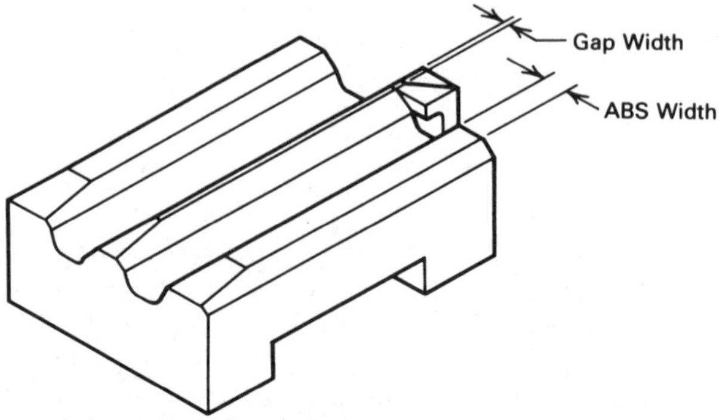

FIGURE 1–7
Winchester heads are built into aerodynamic foils, called *sliders*.

about the problems of loading the heads, as you do with floppies. The characteristics of the air bearing, such as the height to which it lifts the head, are a direct function of the aerodynamic design of the slider.

When the disk isn't moving, the heads actually rest on a specified part of the disk surface, called the *landing zone*. The disk surface is lubricated to reduce the friction when the heads touch the disk, and the drive never stores any data in the landing zone—just in case there is some media damage. When the spindle starts to turn, a cushion of air builds up under the slider, lifting it to its operating altitude. The heads actually take off, climbing to their normal flying height.

Even will all this care, the action of the heads taking off and landing does sometimes stir up some of the oxide particles from the disk's surface. If they lodge in the wrong place, these particles could present a problem. But a constant positive air flow through a particle filter traps those particles adequately.

Contaminants are a constant problem in all disk drives. They can sit on a disk surface and, when the head passes over them, get caught between the head and disk surface. As the media spins, the contaminant scratches the surface of the disk or pits the head. Normally, the only way to prevent this is to keep the head sufficiently high over the disk's surface so that the contaminants aren't a problem. By sealing the head/disk assembly and reducing the possibility that contaminants can get onto the disk's surface, a Winchester drive can allow the head to pass much closer to the disk's surface without sacrificing the drive's reliability.

It doesn't do any good to keep contaminants out of a sealed head/disk assembly if the environment is already dirty, however. To ensure that the disk drive starts off life with a good chance at success, the assembly is put together in a clean room, such as Shugart Corporation's facility shown in Figure 1–8. The particulate count in the room's air determines the grading of the clean room.

If you need higher densities than provided by a conventional Winchester head, there's another design choice. The state-of-the-art Winchester drives on the market use heads made with the same photolithic techniques that are used to manufacture semiconductor devices. These are called *thin-film heads*. The thin-film head has an electromagnet affixed to the end of the slider platform, as shown in Figure 1–9. This slider and the electromagnet's core are both made of ferrite, just as the clumsier toroidal head's core was.

Courtesy of Shugart Corp.

FIGURE 1–8
Building critical disk parts in special clean rooms ensures reliability.

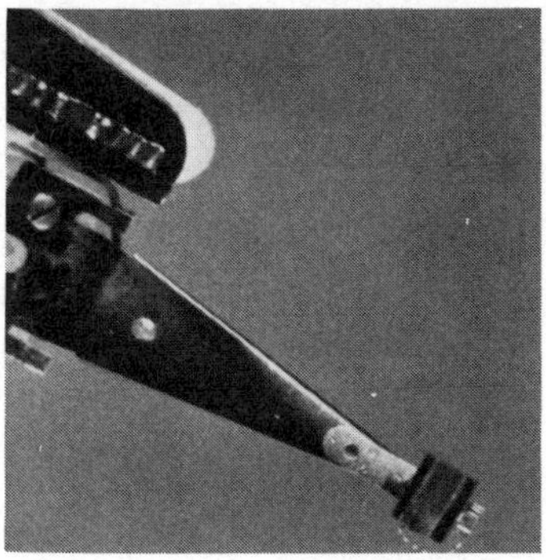

Courtesy of National Micronetics Inc.

FIGURE 1–9
Thin-film heads offer higher recording densities than do ferrite heads.

Because of the tight control a manufacturer using semiconductor technology has over the process, thin-film heads offer much narrower gaps than other types of heads. In fact, the simplest capacity upgrade a manufacturer can make to a disk is to move from ferrite heads to thin-film heads. Thin-film heads are made in three steps:

1. Wafers containing multiple heads are made using semiconductor technologies.
2. Wafers are made into sliders.
3. Sliders are assembled into finished slider/flexure assemblies.

There are two basic types of sliders being used currently: the trimaran, or three-rail head and the two-rail head. All conventional ferrite heads have taken one of these shapes. The trimaran has two outside rails and a center wedge that corresponds to the track width. Thin-film heads tend to use the two-rail design. This approach lets a disk manufacturer use either rail as the read/write head and thus get much closer to the outside edges of the disk surface. More of the disk surface is reachable.

There are several types of slider/flexure assemblies as well. Table 1–1 illustrates the characteristics of some of these assemblies. Each assembly is suitable for use in a particular application. You need to pick the assembly that furnishes the proper head technology (e.g., thin film), the proper flying height for the media, and the necessary radial and linear recording densities.

The smaller sliders, such as the minislider shown in Figure 1–10 (page 16), are coming into widespread use because they have lower mass and are more stable in flight than other slider designs. This means that they can safely fly lower—there's little danger of an air turbulence causing a head crash. And they feature heads which provide 600 to 800 tpi radial densities and 8000+ fci linear densities. It easily becomes possible to think of 5.25-in. rigid disks with 26M bytes of data stored on each disk surface.

TABLE 1–1
A sample of slider/flexure specifications

Type of Technology	*Tracks Per Inch*	*Bits Per Inch*	*Approximate Minimum Flying Height (μin.)*	*Minimum Resolution (%)*	*Type of Erase*	*Typical Disk Speeds (rpm)*
3348 Winchester	300	5800	20	75	None	3000
3350 Winchester	480	6400	20	65	None	3600
3350 Winchester Double Density	960	6400	20	65	None	3600
8-in. Winchester	450-960 typ.	6400-9420 typ.	19	60	None	3600
5¼-in. Winchester	255-345 typ.	7690-9625 typ.	19	60	None	3600
5¼-in. Winchester Composite	460	9000	14	75	None	3400
8-in. Winchester Composite	740	9000	15	70	None	3600
14-in. Winchester Composite	712-960	10000	15	65	None	2400
3370 Thin-Film	635	12134 (Encoded) 8090 FCI	13	90	None	2964
3375 Thin-Film	800	12134 (Encoded) 8090 FCI	13	90	None	2964
3380 Thin-Film	800	15200 (Encoded) 10133 FCI	12	90	None	3620

Let's take a close look at the performance a slider/flexure assembly offers. One minislider, the Model 3377-100 HGA slider from National Micronetics Inc., for example, has a flying height of 10 to 14 μin. on thin-film media and 13 to 17 μin. on oxide media. Intended for use in 5.25-in. rigid disk drives rotating the media at 3600 rpm, the slider can have a gap width as narrow as 700 μin. Another minislider,

FIGURE 1–10
The minislider provides high storage capacities on 5.25-in. disk drives.

Courtesy of Cogito Systems Corp.

the Model 33800, from Applied Magnetics, has a track width of 984 ±40 μin., supporting a radial density of about 800 tpi and flies at 12.5 ±1.5 μin. It expects to see a disk rotating at 3620 rpm.

The importance of the disk rotation will make more sense when we get into a discussion of the data transfer rate. But it also has to do with the head's ability to read and write data at a certain speed. If a head can write data at 9000 bpi (bits per inch), for example, and expects the disk to rotate at 3600 rpm, then it is designed to read and write data at a velocity determined by

$$\text{read/write rate} = \text{rotation (in./sec)} \times \text{density (bpi)}$$

Or, in the case of our example, 3600 rpm for a 5.25-in. disk translates into

$$\frac{3600 \text{ rpm}}{60 \text{ sec/min}} = 60 \text{ rev/sec}$$

$$\begin{aligned} \text{velocity (ips)} &= 60 \text{ rev/sec} \times 6.28 \text{ in. (inner track length)} \\ &= 376.8 \text{ ips} \end{aligned}$$

The first design consideration, therefore, is whether or not this velocity matches your drive's specifications. In a 14-in. Winchester drive, for example, the inner track length would be at least 31.4 in., giving a velocity of 1884 ips at the same disk rotation speed. A typical 14-in. Winchester rotates at 2400 rpm, however, giving a velocity of 1256 ips. The difference in speed plays a significant role in the head's flying stability.

The next concern is the rate at which the head can read and write. If the linear density is 9000 bpi, then, according to the first set of calculations, the head should have no trouble reading and writing at

$$9000 \text{ bpi} \times 376.8 \text{ ips} = 3{,}391{,}200 \text{ bps}$$

If you exceed this rate of about 3.5M bps, you'll have to determine if the head can handle data at the faster speed without problems. And the 14-in. Winchester does exceed this specification. At 1256 ips, the read/write rate is

$$1256 \text{ ips} \times 9000 \text{ bpi} = 11{,}304{,}000 \text{ bps}$$

This transfer rate is, to say the least, significantly higher than what the head specification implies is allowable—by almost four times. But that doesn't necessarily rule out the head technology. Other combinations of linear density and rotation speed might bring the drive into line with the specifications. Understanding the interaction of these specifications will help you determine if a drive vendor is pushing the technology too hard, or if the firm is simply taking advantage of the good things that the state-of-the-art technology provides.

2 The Mechanics

Our discussion of disk drives and the technologies that make them work has just begun. It isn't enough to gain an understanding of the electronics of disk drives and then assume that you know how they work. Disk drives, fortunately or unfortunately, depending on how you feel about moving parts, are electromechanical devices. And the mechanical portion of the drive is vitally important to its overall performance.

The mechanics of a drive include the hardware needed to perform two basic disk operations: They position the heads radially (over the desired track) for writing and reading data, and they rotate the media—turn the spindle to position the data (linearly) under the heads so that it can be read. But how does the drive do all this, and how much of it does the host computer have to control? In this chapter we will take a look at the answer for various disk drive types—including both floppy and rigid disks.

Besides the two tasks we've already mentioned, the drive's mechanics do perform several other important functions, such as shock absorption, cooling, and air filtration, and we will discuss them in detail later on. But these first two mechanical operations are fundamental to the basic operation of all disk drives, whereas the others tend to be extras, albeit important extras. They contribute to the drive's reliability and ruggedness, but have no direct bearing on the way the drive works from a system point of view.

POSITIONING THE HEADS

Before the heads can read or write data, they have to be in position over the proper track. The job of the head-positioning mechanism, one of the more critical and sophisticated contrivances you'll find inside the drive, is to position the heads *radially*, or along the radius of the media. When it comes to positioning heads, there are two basic schools of thought: move the heads to where the track should be or find the track you are looking for. In system control terminology these two head-positioning alternatives are known, respectively, as open-loop and closed-loop positioning systems. Each offers unique advantages and disadvantages for your system.

The basic idea of radial positioning is that the drive will be told, by the host computer, that it is to move the head to a particular track where it is to look for a particular bit of information. This is known as a *seek* operation, since the drive must seek the appropriate track.

In a simple system—one in which the disk peripheral has virtually no intelligence of its own—the host computer even keeps track of which track the drive is currently reading and simply tells the drive how far to move to get to the next track. This is the open-loop system. It is called *open loop* because the feedback loop, which typifies a control system, is incomplete, or open. No information comes back from the system to the controller.

The open-loop system has the virtue of being the simplest and the least costly to manufacture in quantity. That is its first and primary advantage. It seeks tracks blindly. A stepper motor moves the head a predetermined distance from one track to the next. The stepper moves three steps (or perhaps six steps, in some systems) to move over three tracks.

An open-loop stepper motor is the most prevalent way of positioning heads. In fact, the terminology for positioning heads reflects this technique. We talk of stepping to a certain track. The assumption behind this design is that if a stepper motor can move the head a fixed distance consistently (if each step pulse sent to the stepper motor moves the heads the same distance toward the disk's hub), then that step represents the distance between tracks. The uniformity of the step, obviously, is a direct consequence of the accuracy of the stepper motor. But accuracy costs; so, at low densities many manufacturers will opt for less expensive motors. At high densities the higher-priced motors become mandatory.

The drawback to open-loop systems is that, in order to guarantee the drive's performance, the stepper motor must be consistent in both its step sizes and stepping speed. Even at its best, the stepper motor works as if the tracks are always in exactly the same place, and we know that they are not. This limits the amount of information that can be practically stored on a disk.

GETTING OUT OF ROUND

The stepper motor approach assumes that the media (or the tracks written on the media, at least) will be reasonably round. The tolerance for what is reasonable depends greatly on the radial density—the number of tracks you put on the disk. The more tracks there are per inch of disk surface, the less media distortion or step variation the drive can allow. That is, the less reasonable, or tolerant, the drive can be.

In order to reliably retrieve information, when it reads data the stepper motor must put the heads in more or less the same spot that it did when it wrote it. In low-density recording, such as floppy single density (48 tpi), you'll seldom see any problem at all. But as the track density increases, it is more likely that positioning problems will crop up. In an open-loop system there isn't any way to compensate for changes over time.

If the positioner doesn't operate reliably, the problem may be troublesome to isolate. You'll find it hard to tell exactly what went wrong. You just won't be able to get the disk to read the data you know is stored on it. The term for what you'll be experiencing is *off-track read error,* not that it does much good to name it. If the error is large enough, the disk might go beyond not reading and conceivably read the wrong track.

Thus, under the best of circumstances (when the media is perfect), the open-loop system works exactly as well or as poorly as its stepper motor does. Under the worst of circumstances, media distortion also plays a role. The only motor specification that has any bearing on the drive's ability to position the heads accurately is that of the tolerance of the steps. When you pulse it, the stepper will rotate a specific number of degrees.

If the worst-case positioning job that the motor can do puts the head close enough to the track's centerline that the read head can retrieve the information, the operation is successful. If the worst-case positioning job puts the head very far from the track's centerline, the drive won't be able to recover the stored information. It's that simple. It's also that fatal.

SPECIFYING THE POSITIONER

Typical of open-loop positioners is the Fasflex actuator that Shugart Corporation uses in various forms in its floppy and hard disk drives. (You'll notice that, for the purposes of this book, the terms *hard, rigid,* and Winchester become interchangeable. Although all Winchesters are rigid disks, the converse is not true. But, at the rate Winchesters are displacing the competition, it soon will be.)

The Fasflex actuator used in floppy disks (Figure 2–1) couples the stepper motor's shaft to the head assembly with a band made of spring metal. The tension of the metal band helps eliminate the hysteresis that can slow you down when you want the head to move. That is, if the capstan simply turned against the head carriage, forcing it in or out, there would be a natural lag as the carriage overcame its own inertia. The spring metal *preloads* the carriage. This means that it keeps the head carriage under stress so that it is poised to move. Then, when the capstan turns, the carriage moves immediately. This helps give the drive better (faster) seek times than it would otherwise have. Essentially, preloading is a matter of taking the sloppiness out of the mechanics of the positioning mechanism.

Although the actuator's performance primarily controls the seek time, the specification we usually use in comparing

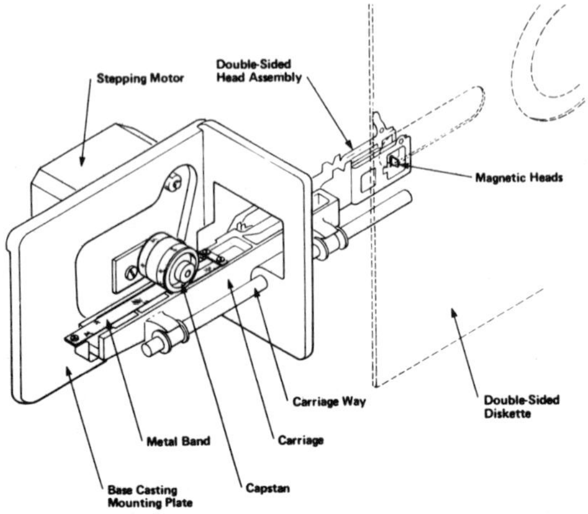

FIGURE 2–1
A stepper motor, coupled to the head assembly with a metal band, moves a floppy drive's heads in and out.

Courtesy of Shugart Corp.

disk drives to each other is the *average access time*. A disk drive's access time is the time it takes for the drive to retrieve the data from the moment the host computer asks for it. The average amount of time it takes to locate a track is the drive's average access time.

Two specifications affect the average access time: the seek time (the time it takes to find a track) and the *latency time*. The latency time is the time it takes the drive to position the data you want under the heads once it has found the right track. The worst thing that can happen to you is that the data will have just passed under the heads and you must wait an entire disk rotation. But, the odds being what they are, you can figure the latency time at half the time of a complete rotation.

In Shugart Corporation's SA200 floppy disk drive, for example, the 5.25-in. diskette rotates at 300 rpm. One rotation, therefore takes 1/300 min, or 200 msec. So we figure the diskette's latency time at 100 msec.

The SA200 has a track-to-track access time of 26 msec. To calculate its average access time, add the track-to-track access time to the settling time (20 msec) and latency time,

or $$26 + 20 + 100 = 146 \text{ msec}$$

In other words, on the average, you can expect the SA200

to take an average of 146 msec to find a particular sector on the disk. The only way it might find data faster would be if it didn't have to change tracks. The settling time, by the way, is dead time that gives the heads a chance to stop bouncing against the media and settle into firm contact for reliable reading and writing. In a case where the drive has to step a large number of tracks, the access time goes way up, however.

A more sophisticated drive from the same manufacturer, the SA810, combines a 3-msec track-to-track access time with 13 msec settling time and 83 msec latency time (360 rpm) to obtain an average access time of 89 msec.

The Fasflex II used in Shugart's Winchester drives provides much the same loading and coupling features as the mechanism used in the floppy drives. This time, however, the head assembly rotates about an offset pivot point rather than moving in and out linearly. This pivoting helps reduce the size of the disk package. It makes more efficient use of space.

A similar actuator system, the positioning system used by Computer Memories in its CM 5000 5.25-in. Winchester drive (Figure 2–2), illustrates the rotation concept. The preloaded ball bearings provide smooth movement about the pivot point with a load of two to six heads on the arm.

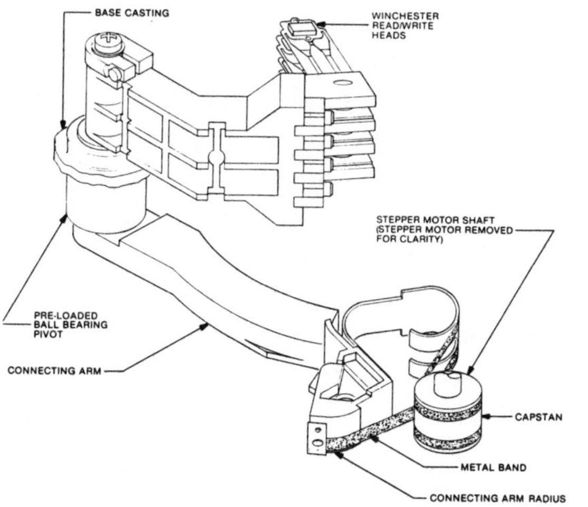

Courtesy of Computer Memories, Inc.

FIGURE 2–2
Pivoting the head arm's motion around a preloaded ball bearing provides performance in a small space.

Each time the drive issues a step pulse, the stepper motor moves 0.9 degree—enough to move the heads one track. And the stepper must step quickly. The speed at which it can step will determine the time it takes a disk to access information. In the normal step mode a direction logic line determines whether the motor will step in (toward the hub) or out (away from the hub). A step pulse actuates the step. You can issue step pulses to the actuator with as few as 3 msec between pulses. Each step pulse must last at least 500 nsec long.

If you run the step pulses closer together, the positioner automatically shifts into a buffered mode. Whenever the step pulses are closer together than 200 μsec (but more than 8 μsec apart) they are stored in a buffer. After the last step pulse is stored, the heads begin stepping the desired number of tracks. When they reach the desired track, the SEEK COMPLETE signal goes true (within 216 msec).

For its newest models of half-height 5.25-in. Winchester drives, Shugart has introduced the Fasflex IV rotary actuator, a compact version of the actuator used in the larger drives.

In spite of the different configurations of the rigid disk positioner mechanisms, they remain simple open-loop systems. If the media distortion becomes too great, or the track density too high, they won't be able to write and retrieve data reliably.

Most open-loop systems have the stepper motor located in a place that will provide some degree of thermal isolation from the head assembly. The stepper motor will generate much of the heat in the drive, and you don't want that heat coupled directly to the head assembly where it could cause damage. There's enough heat generated in a disk as it is without adding to it unnecessarily.

In looking at the drive specifications, especially for high-capacity drives, you'll sometimes see references to the number of *cylinders* that the drive has, rather than tracks. The term cylinder is used when the drive has several read/write heads. All of the data tracks under the heads (all the data that it can read without moving the heads) are said to be part of the same cylinder. If the drive has three platters, with read/write heads on five surfaces (and the sixth contains servo data), the cylinder 0 would include track 0 on all five surfaces. The track-to-track access time within a cylinder should be 0 msec.

Open-loop systems have been around for some time now and aren't likely to go away any time soon. In summary they offer the following:

Advantages:

- Low initial cost
- Lower upkeep costs (servo data on media not required)
- Simple, reliable design

Disadvantages:

- Poor tolerance for track distortion
- Low track densities

Closing the Loop

Closed-loop systems offer disk drives something else altogether in terms of design and potential performance. They require more sophisticated positioning mechanisms which can provide both large and small adjustments to the track position and a feedback mechanism to let the positioner know where it is.

Some vendors use voice-coil positioners which can literally put the heads anywhere on the disk surface. Rather than stepping in discrete increments across the surface, they move linearly and continuously across its surface. These are analog positioners and the exact amount of movement is a function of the voltage applied to the positioner.

Other designs use stepper motors which have a variety of step sizes. Large steps get the heads quickly to the approximate position of the track and the smaller steps fine tune the position to center the heads over the track. A variation on this approach involves two steppers: one provides the large (coarse) adjustments and the other takes care of the small (fine) movements that it takes to put the heads onto the exact track center.

Regardless of the motor technology used, all closed-loop systems provide some kind of feedback that tells the positioner how well the heads are positioned over the track. The control keeps working to ensure that the optimum position is maintained.

The logic behind going to all the trouble that closed-loop positioners require is that accurate positioning allows you to count on the head being positioned precisely over the track's centerline. The track can therefore be narrower, allowing you to make more efficient use of the disk space physically available. You can put the tracks closer together without any danger that the drive will read the wrong track. And, the narrower you can make the tracks, the closer you can squeeze them together, and the more tracks the surface can contain.

So why don't all drives use closed-loop positioners? Because they require some careful design before they work properly. There's quite a bit that can go wrong in any electronic system, and the more complex you make the system, the harder it will be to get it working exactly right. Besides, closed-loop systems add substantially to the cost of the drive. And the media must be specially prepared with prerecorded servo data.

A basic two-stepper motor closed-loop system, as illustrated by the block diagram shown in Figure 2–3, requires that there be some information prerecorded on the disk to tell the drive where the head is positioned—not only which track it is reading, but also how far it is from the centerline of that track. This required information track is known as a *servo track*. Once the disk drive manufacturer writes it on the disk surface, it remains there for the life of the drive.

There are two basic methods of putting servo information on a disk. You can dedicate an entire disk surface to the servo information. The head that reads that surface does nothing but provide positioning information—both track and sector identification. This has the advantage of being a rather straightforward way of doing things. Many manufacturers, especially those who stack as many as eight disk platters (16 disk surfaces) in one drive, prefer this approach.

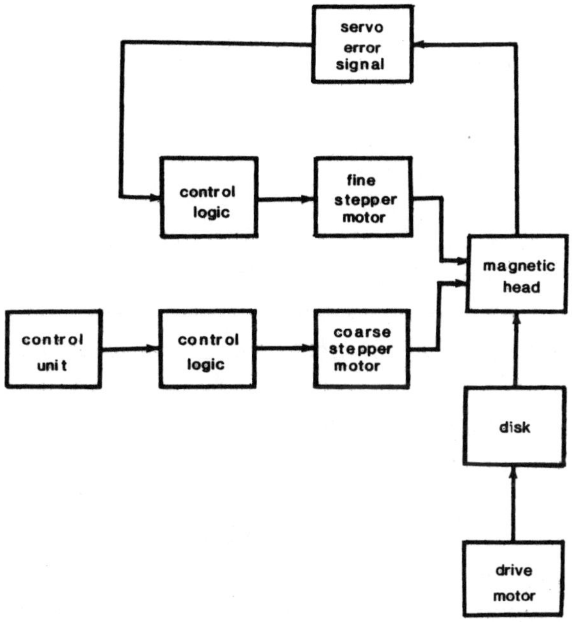

FIGURE 2–3
Closed-loop head-positioning systems read a servo track to find out what track they are on and to find the center of that track.

They can afford to give up an entire disk surface to providing servo information. And, to get the maximum capacity from the drive, the dedicated servo is perhaps the only way to go. The continuous position monitoring that the dedicated servo provides keeps the heads constantly on the track's center, allowing the designer to squeeze the tracks together as much as possible.

USING SERVO DATA

The servo information is typically written on the media by the drive manufacturer—it must, after all, reflect the characteristics of the drive system, not just the disk. But the case of removable media proves different. Here the servo tracks can also be provided by some media manufacturers. But then, the drive system must conform to these tracks completely.

A typical approach involves placing permanent synchronization areas at equal points about the servo surface, cutting it up as if it were a pie. When the servo head reads this regular pattern, it knows that the next data it sees will be a servo byte that will contain the information needed to position the heads properly. In a system termed the *quadrature*

FIGURE 2–4
Track-following embedded servos include the servo bursts in each sector.

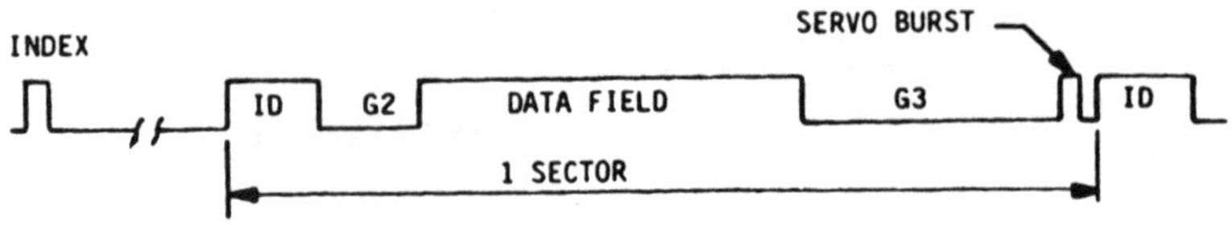

system the track identification data is stored as a series of four double-bit position signals. One set of bits straddles the track evenly, one set of bits is located on each side of the track, and the fourth set doesn't touch the track at all. If the head is centered over the track, the bit pair that straddles the track will produce a maximum pulse in each direction; the two offset pairs will produce weaker signals; the completely offset pair shouldn't even be read. Any other pattern tells the positioner that it is off track. The precise pattern will tell it which direction it is off, to boot.

But, if you only have one platter in your drive, giving up half of your storage space to position information can prove unpleasant. There's another way. Two other ways, in fact.

When you need servo data to make the performance cut-off, but can't spare the space to record it, the solution might be the track-following *embedded servo*. An embedded servo is one that is placed between data sectors of each track. This means that the information is available only sporadically. DMA Systems uses an embedded servo to ensure that a drive will read data on any removable cartridge. Each track contains 33 sectors, and each sector contains 26 bytes of servo information ahead of the data.

Drivetec uses an embedded servo to pack up to 3.3M bytes of data on an 8-in. floppy diskette. The format of each

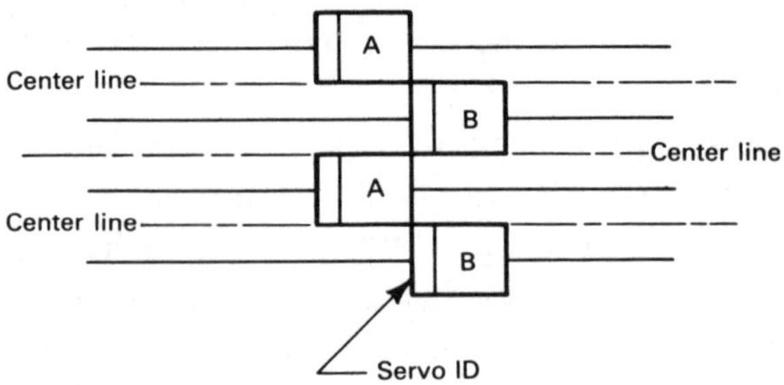

FIGURE 2–5
Two servo bursts, one offsetting each side of the track's centerline, provide position information.

Courtesy of Drivetec Inc.

track on the diskette is arranged as shown in Figure 2–4. This system acts like a simpler version of the quadrature servo approach, except that it works only in two dimensions. Each track has two servo bursts: one offset from the centerline to one side, the other to the opposite side, as shown in Figure 2–5. The feedback loop seeks until the amplitudes of the two bursts it is reading are equal. By definition, equalizing the amplitude of the two bursts will put the heads on the track's centerline. And track following is important if you intend to store 192 tpi on an 8-in. floppy diskette. There isn't much room for error.

Yet another firm is using a closed-loop system to keep floppies competitive in their storage capacity. Amlyn has developed what might be termed an organic closed loop—it's more like biofeedback than it is a conventional closed-loop servo. In this innovative technique the microprocessor-controlled actuator references its step sizes to a strip of mylar with stripes drawn on it. You can see this setup in Figure 2–6. The mylar has 10 marks for each step and is treated so that it has exactly the same thermal and hydroscopic characteristics as the floppy diskette. As the diskette expands, the mylar expands, and the steps that the actuator makes per track become proportionally larger. Using this technique, Amlyn puts 170 tpi on a diskette surface. Although this approach certainly isn't a servo system, embed-

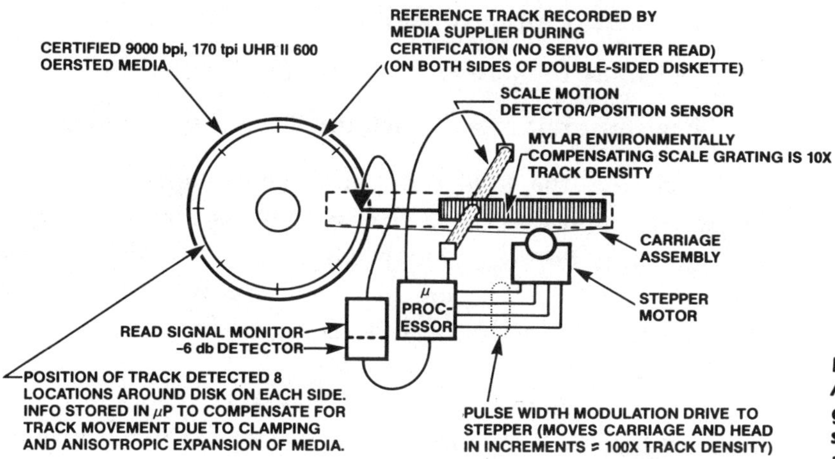

Courtesy of Amlyn.

FIGURE 2–6
A mylar strip provides a gauge of how much the step size should be adjusted to compensate for changes in the media.

ded or otherwise, it does qualify as a closed-loop system. As such it will take care of a great deal of the read/write errors due to media deformation (variations in the surface) and spindle runout (eccentricities in the spindle's rotation).

The closed-loop technique provides drives that offer a different set of advantages and disadvantages than open-loop drives. They are as follows:

Advantages:

- Accommodate higher track densities, therefore higher storage capacities
- Tolerate media distortion
- Can offer faster positioning

Disadvantages:

- Higher initial cost
- Require media containing servo data
- More complex design

TURNING THE SPINDLE

You can't read the data on the platter unless the media passes under the heads. You have to turn the spindle that the disks are connected to. There are three important things to remember about the motors that drive spindles in rigid disk drives:

1. They must turn the disk at a uniform speed.
2. They must rotate with a minimum of wobble.
3. They must not rotate when the drive is powered off.

Of course, the first two points apply equally well to floppy and rigid disks, but the last item is unique to rigid disk drives. A floppy has its heads clear of the disk surface when the power is off, and the media has usually been removed from the drive as well. A fixed disk drive works much differently.

Because a Winchester drive's heads rest on the disk's surface when the power is off, you don't want the disk spinning around during shipping or rough handling. It could cause a disk crash. To make sure that this doesn't happen, most Winchesters come with a spindle lock of some sort. In the case of Shugart Corporation's SA700 series drives, the spindle lock consists of a mechanical brake that is deactivated whenever power is applied. But when power is lost, the spindle stops turning quickly.

In the case of removable cartridge drives, it is important that the spindle stop turning as soon as possible so that you can change cartridges. But you don't want the heads to land on the disk surface inside the cartridge. You want them to retract from the cartridge. Cartridge drives, therefore, need both brakes and a system for retracting the heads before the drive stops rotating.

Dynamic electrical braking decelerates the spindle nicely. Basically, this means that the motor will act as a generator after power is removed. The act of generating power produces a reverse magnetic field that acts against the motor, slowing it down quickly. And the power the motor generates guarantees that there will be enough juice available to retract the heads.

MAINTAINING SPINDLE SPEED

The accuracy with which you will need to control the spindle speed is a function of the recording scheme. But, the higher the density of data on the disk, the more important the spindle speed. Most high-capacity drives use microprocessor-based motor controllers and DC brushless motors to keep the spindle speed within 0.1 percent. Some manufacturers even specify the direction of any errors. Shugart Corporation's SA700, for example, has its spindle speed specified at 3600 rpm, with a maximum speed of 3600 rpm and a minimum of 3528 rpm.

The internal microprocessor handles all of these supervisory functions nicely. Any deviations will usually be mechanical ones rather than electrical. In fact, the job is so trivial for a microprocessor that in some drives the same controller will, in its spare time, handle the head-positioning system and other housekeeping chores such as keeping a record of disk errors and performing cyclic redundancy checks (CRC).

CLEANING THE AIR

In order to achieve the remarkable performance and storage capacities that current disks offer, the heads must come as low as within 10 μin. of the disk surface. Any debris on the disk surface could damage the heads, disk surface, or both. To take care of such problems the drives are assembled in a clean room. But what do you do about contaminants that leak into a removable cartridge? Can you guarantee the head/disk assembly's integrity?

Winchester disk cartridge manufacturers, such as DMA Systems, go to great lengths to keep foreign matter out of their disks. Special seals around every opening make the cartridge an airtight fit. But they aren't quite certain about the drive's ability to keep doing that successfully. The firm suggests that cartridge drives (such as the DMA Systems drive shown in Figure 2–7) be used only in office environments, that cartridges be kept in their protective sleeves when not in use, that users not tamper with the cartridges or the inside portion of the drive, and that the cartridge not be exposed to oily or sticky substances. But this might not be enough. So they added some important housekeeping hardware.

The housekeeping hardware consists of a complete closed-loop air-cleaning system. There's that term again. This time it is the flow of air, rather than of electrons, that runs in a closed loop. Below the disk, contained in the drive

FIGURE 2–7
Removable cartridges run the risk of introducing contaminants into the head/disk assembly.

Courtesy of DMA Systems.

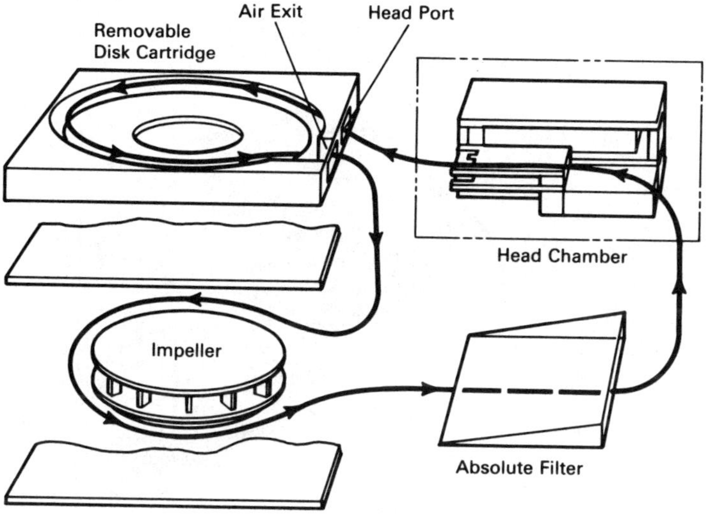

Courtesy of DMA Systems.

FIGURE 2–8
A closed-loop clean air system removes particles before they can do any damage.

itself, is an impeller that is powerful enough to draw the entire volume of air into the drive through the recirculating filter once every second. As you see in the airflow diagram shown in Figure 2–8, the airflow includes every part of the assembly to remove particles that might have gotten into the assembly when you changed cartridges.

When you turn on the spindle motor, the impeller that it drives in turn creates a positive pressure against an absolute filter which removes any particles large enough to cause problems. The positive air pressure also ensures that any air leaks will be outward from the sealed disk assembly, rather than inward into it, thus making sure that additional particles aren't sucked into the disk assembly.

The absolute filters are specified in terms of the absolute size of particles which they will allow to pass through them. One manufacturer of removable cartridge drives specifies that the filter in its removable cartridge drive will trap particles larger than 0.3 micron. The size of the particles that must be filtered will depend, of course, on the flying height of the drive's heads. Other than this pragmatic, and extremely empirical, determination, you can't really say that there is any *best* size of filter or maximum allowable particle size.

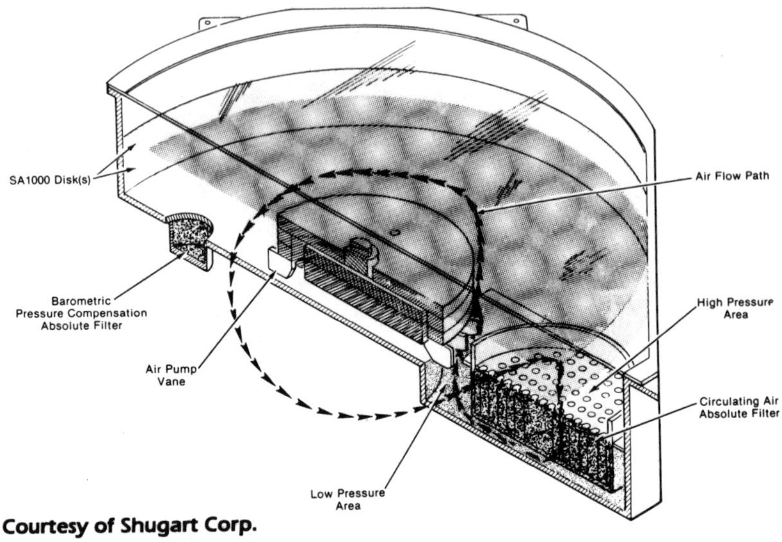

FIGURE 2–9
A fixed drive's filtration system shouldn't have to work as hard as one in a cartridge.

Courtesy of Shugart Corp.

Fixed drives tend to be less demanding of their air-cleaning systems than removable cartridge systems are. The assumption made in their manufacture, and it is a reasonable one, is that most of the contaminants that you have to worry about in removable media are introduced when you are changing cartridges. In the sealed environment of the fixed disk, the only debris should be that kicked up when the heads take off and land.

Even in this less demanding environment you'll find extensive filtering. The airflow diagram shown in Figure 2–9 illustrates one such filtration system.

Regardless of the system, however, every time the spindle motor starts up, the head/disk assembly gets purged. Any contaminants present in the assembly are forced through the filter and trapped. The heads and disk surfaces in the head/disk assembly stay clean enough to prevent damage.

Airflow through the head/disk assembly has one other important function—it keeps the temperature down. A 14-in. disk platter spinning in air can dissipate as much as 50 W. Multiply this output by several platters, and you'll see what begins to happen to the temperature in an assembly housing a high-capacity disk stack.

High temperatures increase the stress on any integrated circuits that might be in the assembly, such as the read/write amplifiers or data separator. And, if you use thin-film heads, bear in mind that these are also semiconductor devices. A few disks spinning might not raise the temperature enough to make the chips fail, but prolonged high temperatures can certainly shorten the lifespan of every component in the drive.

Maintaining a healthy airflow throughout the disk pack can help keep the temperatures under control. It can certainly prevent the drive from developing any hot spots. The temperature will remain uniform throughout. But, as with so many disk specifications, it's hard to call out some "good" value for temperature. As a rule of thumb, the more cooling the better. But remember, extra cooling costs extra dollars.

3 The Media

You can't consider a study of a storage device complete unless it includes an examination of the storage media—the disk itself, in this case. The capabilities of the media reflect directly on the capabilities of the drive, and therefore on the overall system performance. Regardless of the form the media takes, floppy diskette or rigid disk, the major system requirements remain the same: the media must store information cheaply and reliably.

In order to simplify the discussion of media, it breaks, as it logically should, into two major segments: the first addresses floppy diskettes and the second, rigid disks. Although both are magnetic media, the technologies involved in the two media types are sufficiently different to warrant the division. Furthermore, the standards of performance vary from one to the other. What might prove an acceptable reliability level for a floppy disk won't suffice for a rigid disk.

Even within the rigid disk category, we want to make a distinction between two media types. Some drives use oxide-coated media, and some use a plated media. There are different price/performance considerations associated with each, but there is an intermixing of the two. You can use plated media where oxide-coated media will do the trick, but it won't work the other way around, as you'll see. Where plated media is needed, only plated media will do. Understanding the pluses and minuses of each will help us see why this is the case.

FLOPPY DISKETTES

A typical floppy diskette, such as any of TDK's 5.25- and 8-in. diskettes shown in Figure 3–1, features not only the same magnetic characteristics as magnetic tape, it also has much the same physical structure. It's constructed of sheets of a neutral base material that have been covered with a magnetic coating. The coating is then cut, much like cookies are, into circular disks which are lubricated and put into protective jackets which, at least in the case of 5.25-in. and 8-in. floppies, are made of cardboard or vinyl.

The diskette's jacket serves two important purposes. The first purpose is simple physical protection. The jacket protects the magnetic coating from damage when you handle the media—within limits. Except in the case of some microfloppies, which have rigid plastic jackets, as exhibited by the specification for the 3.5-in. floppy shown in Figure 3–2, floppies will withstand very little in the way of mishandling. But as long as you are handling them properly (gently) the jacket provides adequate protection.

The microfloppy's rigid jacket furnishes more than protection. The positioning hole and centering hub ensure

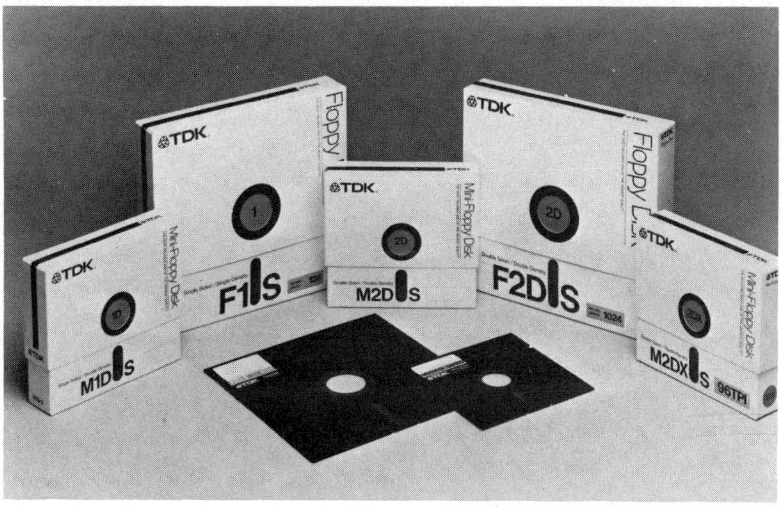

Courtesy of TDK Electronics Corp.

FIGURE 3–1
Members of TDK's floppy diskette family come with soft jackets for protection.

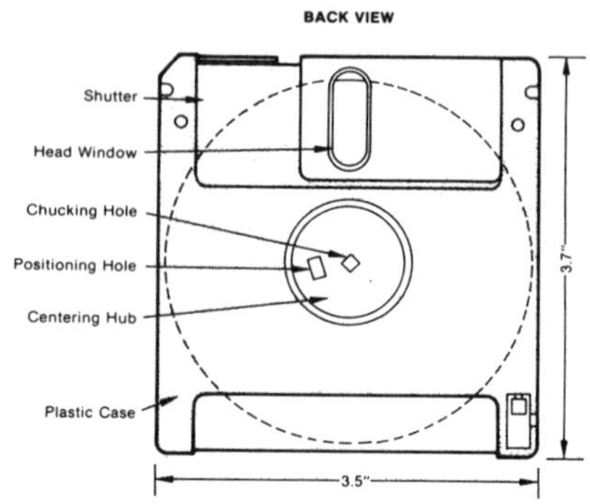

FIGURE 3–2
The microfloppy's jacket is rigid and features a shutter that automatically closes when you remove the diskette from the drive.

tracking accuracy. The automatic shutter closes to keep contaminants off the diskette's surface.

But not all microfloppies use the rigid jacket. In order to keep prices down and to conform to the standards set by larger floppies, companies such as Dysan and Tabor support 3.25-in. floppies that have a traditional soft jacket, as shown by the Dysan Flex Diskette in Figure 3–3.

The jacket's second function is cleaning. Most diskette jackets have a special liner that stays in contact with the disk surface. It is there to remove microscopic debris from the surface that might cause read/write errors or damage to the diskette surface or heads. The liner is typically a nonwoven, nonshedding cloth that is either thermally bonded (Accutrack thermally bonds liners to the jacket, e.g.) or spot-welded (as is TDK's line) to the jacket material.

FIGURE 3–3
Some microfloppy diskettes use the conventional soft jacket of larger floppies.

Courtesy of Dysan Corp.

There is a third, somewhat less important, role that the jacket plays. You can use the jacket for labeling the diskette, both physically and electrically. Electronically you can protect information on the diskette. The notches on the jacket (shown in Figure 3–4) serve two purposes: they relieve stress (help keep the diskette from creasing) and indicate whether a diskette should be written or not. By covering over the write-enable notch (or opening the write-protect notch on some diskettes), you can make sure that the system won't write on the diskette, otherwise you can accidentally erase important information.

Physically marking the diskette requires a place on which to mark it. Obviously you couldn't put anything at all on the floppy's surface—it would keep it from working. You aren't even supposed to touch the magnetic surface. But you can put a label on the jacket. This might not sound technically significant, but ask any computer user with more than 10 diskettes to keep track of how easy it would be to find a particular file or database without that feature.

The Construction

In the case of floppy disks the neutral base material is the same as it is for magnetic tape—plastic. The coating is usually made with finely ground red oxide particles as the magnetic material, contained in a binder. It is this coating, actually the particles in the coating, which will retain the magnetic fields and thus give the disk its ability to store

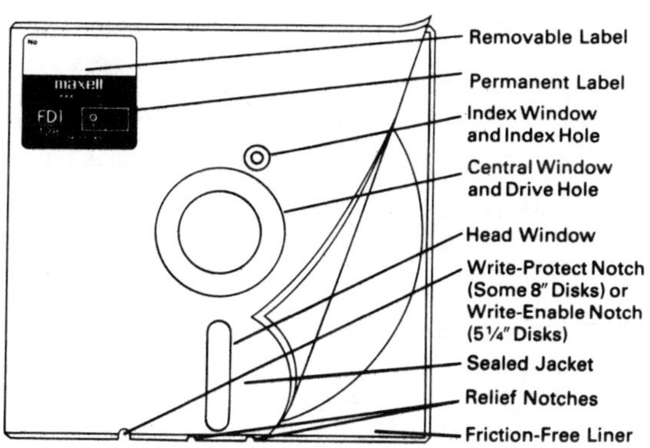

Courtesy of Maxell Corp. of America.

FIGURE 3–4
Notches in the diskette jacket provide stress relief and indicate whether or not a diskette is protected from erasure.

data. Thus, the performance of the coating, in terms of the density of flux reversals (measured in flux reversals per inch or frpi) that it can accept and retain, gives us one of the major limits of the disk subsystem's ultimate performance.

The Disk Coating

Because the magnetic characteristics of the oxide particles—the size of the domains in particular—define the disk's storage capability, and are, in effect, the storage medium (rather than the disk), you need to understand something about the nature of these particles before you can adequately evaluate the various disk technologies available today and the ones certain to come tomorrow.

The red oxide (gamma iron oxide) particles that coat the diskette surface are typically less than 1 micron long (less than 40 μin.) and needle shaped (icicular). In its crystalline form the red oxide has a spinel structure (cubic symmetry) that is much like that of magnetite—the material that is widely used in magnetic cores. The size and shape of these particles help determine the maximum density with which you can store information on the media. For some applications the particles may be ground spherically, but the use of icicular particles lets you orient the particles in the direction they will align when magnetized. At a particular moment in the coating process, the media manufacturer subjects the coating to a magnetic field. This magnetization process produces a small, but very real, increase in performance. Regardless of the process employed, ideally, each particle will behave magnetically as an individual domain. If you can make the media behave that way, you'll get the best possible performance from the media.

When you get down to the basics, information storage is actually a matter of controlling the polarity of these particles. The smaller the coating manufacturer can make these domains, the higher the potential disk storage density the coating provides. Improvements in coatings relate directly to an increase in storage capacity. Smaller, more controllable domains can be more tightly packed. A higher density of particles permits a comparable increase in the density of flux reversals. And by definition, the more flux reversals you can store in a given space, the more information the disk can store. Thus, it would seem that the smaller the particles, the better the material. But there is a limit to this logic, a physical limit. Particles smaller than about 200Å in diameter aren't stable single domains at room temperature. They wouldn't retain anything stored (magnetically).

There are various magnetic materials (besides red oxide) being considered and used for disk coatings. Cobalt-modified iron oxide particles, for example, offer a 7 to 11 percent increase in coercivity over pure iron oxide. A division of Kodak, Spin Physics, has introduced a high-density coating that uses such an approach. The firm's Isomax coating uses a 5-micron thick coating of cobalt-enhanced iron oxide that has substantially smaller particle sizes than do conventional floppies. The particles are spherical, rather than conical. As a result, you can control the particle's magnetization both perpendicularly and longitudinally. The Isomax media lets you store up to 40,000 frpi on a floppy diskette. In 1983 the media isn't in full production. It will be a few years before we know if the media will be cost-effective.

And there are other high-performance options. Chromium dioxide (CrO_2) also provides excellent high-density performance. But it is also costly and, unfortunately, much too abrasive for continued use. Most floppies are specified to last several million head passes. Accutrack, for example, intends its diskettes to withstand 12 million passes without disk-related errors or significant wear.

As you can see, there is a lot that goes into picking out the best materials for a diskette. When a disk manufacturer chooses a coating, he must evaluate the material on the basis of both its magnetic properties and its physical characteristics. In part, the magnetic characteristics of the diskette will be determined by the physical properties of the materials. When picking the right particles, for example, it is important to determine how evenly the particles will disperse in the coating solution.

Without an even dispersion of the magnetic particles in the coating solution, you can't count on getting them spread evenly on the diskette. And, without even dispersion, you won't see uniform magnetic properties over the disk's surface. Manufacturers, therefore, must take special care in making the coating preparation and use specially milled ferrous-oxide particles (to ensure a uniform size) and a cross-linked binder (which helps guarantee a smooth surface) to ensure a smooth, well-dispersed coating up to 2.5 microns thick.

Keeping Things Glossy

Magnetic performance isn't the only reason for worrying about how smooth the disk surface is. In a floppy disk drive the heads are actually in contact with the media. No matter how well the process is controlled there will be some friction. And, if there are any foreign particles in the coating, there can be problems. If the particles are softer than the heads, you'll get an error (depending on the size of the particle), but no head wear; if the particles are harder than the material the heads are made from, you'll get severe head wear and an error. This can shorten the life of the head.

The degree of evenness of the dispersion of the magnetic particles over the disk's surface will have a pervasive effect on many performance characteristics, including the disk's erase noise (the amount of noise that the erasing function doesn't eliminate) and the modulation noise. If the dispersion is poor enough, it can cause nonuniformities in the disk's surface, called *dropouts*. Simply defined, a dropout is a portion of the disk surface that can't be recorded on or read. It is unusable. It doesn't matter whether the problem is a cluster of oxide particles or a spot where particles are missing.

Dropouts, if large enough, can produce single-bit errors and interference problems between adjacent pulses on the disk. And single-bit errors, in spite of their innocuous name, can be fatal to the manufacturer's yields. Many of the current media standards define a defective track as one with a missing or an extra bit.

Poor dispersion of the magnetic particles isn't the only thing that can give the media manufacturer trouble. The size of the particles must also be uniform. Particle size must be monitored. If large magnetic particles get mixed in with the small particles, the magnetic characteristics of the recording surface become unpredictable. The heads will write differently over some parts of the disk's surface than others.

Regardless of the cause of a defect, whether it's due to poor dispersion or irregularly sized particles, the specific nature of the problem it causes will depend on the size of the nonuniformity it creates. Basically, if the defect is smaller than one-half of the wavelength of the recorded signal, the problems will come in the form of high noise levels and single-bit errors.

To keep things smooth, therefore, the diskette surface is burnished (which flattens the oxide) and coated with a lubricant to ensure high gloss and low head wear. Manufacturers offer unique and proprietary smoothing operations, lubricants, and different approaches to burnishing, which they feel works best.

However the manufacturer processes the materials, the hoped-for result is pretty much the same—an error-free diskette. To get a better idea of what is needed, let's take a look at some of the desired magnetic properties and how hard it can be to obtain them.

COERCIVITY AND REMANENCE

Among the various magnetic properties that a manufacturer might consider when choosing the right one for a disk, the one all manufacturers are most fond of quoting is the coercivity. Coercivity (or remanence coercivity) is a measure of how well the coating can withstand demagnetizing fields. In a sense, coercivity measures exactly how stubborn the magnetic field on the disk is. But coercive force is a two-way street. It also gives us an idea of how difficult it is to write information on the surface in the first place. And it's a simple relationship. The harder it is to accidentally erase data from the disk with an errant or wayward demagnetizing field, the harder it will be to write something on the disk.

An interesting relationship exists between coercivity and physical hardness. Magnetic materials which are physically very hard, such as steels, tend to have a very high coercivity. They retain their induced magnetic fields. Softer magnetic materials, such as iron, have a low coercivity but a high permeability, that is, they make strong electromagnets but readily lose their induced magnetism. This relationship indicates some of the additional trade-offs that a disk manufacturer might have to deal with. Most hard magnetic materials prove hard to work with.

The significance of coercivity can't be underrated. Floppy disk drives, in particular, subject their media to severe magnetic fields. And these fields, if not taken into account, can make you lose whatever data you've stored on the diskette.

Consider the floppy's environment. Many times the drives are located near, or even in the same cabinet with, video monitors (CRTs) or switching power supplies. The flyback transformer and yoke of the CRT produce time-varying magnetic fields that can interfere with the disk's operation. And the drive itself produces some magnetic fields. In a 5.25-in. floppy disk drive, the head load solenoids and stepper motor can cause nearly as much interference as the CRT. The head load solenoid alone can produce a magnetic flux density of 1.3 G across the read/write head gap. When it comes to data integrity, the drive itself can be its own worst enemy.

The second important magnetic property of a disk coating is its saturation magnetization. This is the actual maximum charge that the coating can absorb. The higher the saturation magnetization level, the larger the signal that the coating stores. Sometimes nonmagnetic properties must take precedence over magnetic ones. To protect the iron particles in coatings from oxidation, they are deliberately surrounded by an oxide layer. This protects them from nonuniform oxidation but also reduces the saturation-magnetization level. But the trade-off is necessary.

All materials that have good magnetic properties don't necessarily make good disk coatings, however. There are always trade-offs between the quality of the particle's magnetic properties and how well it disperses or how uniformly it can be milled. Because we've already seen the problems such irregularities can cause, it's easy to sympathize with the media manufacturer.

MEDIA STANDARDS

The actual coating materials a media manufacturer chooses shouldn't matter very much to you as a user of disks, really. You'll find yourself more concerned with the performance standards that have been developed for the various media. And the media standards, developed by organizations such as ANSI (the American National Standards Institute, Inc.), don't specify the material. Instead, they specify the electromagnetic performance and physical characteristics of the media. They look at the effect and don't care much about the cause.

Consider that workhorse of personal computers, the single-sided, single-density 5.25-in. floppy disk, for example. The performance of this disk media is covered by ANSI document X3.82-1980. The document doesn't specify how the disk should be made. Instead, it defines the allowable abrasivity, roughness, wear resistance, light transmittance (of the index hole), magnetic coating resistivity, flammability, and toxicity. The abrasivity is the characteristic "that results in wear or abrasion of a read/write head or its pressure pad, or both," according to the standard. A detailed test (Appendix E of the standard) determines whether a disk is too abrasive or not.

The media's roughness is simpler to determine. Roughness is usually a function of the coating process. Either the mixture of particles is wrong, the particles themselves aren't ground uniformly, or the coating is put on improperly. If the coating is put on properly, and sets properly, it should be smooth, not lumpy. But no process is perfect. There will undoubtedly be some bumps on the surface. To determine if the bumps will be a problem, look at the surface with a microscope and ensure that the bumps on the surface don't exceed 3 μin. in height. The presence of larger defects indicates poorly made media that can cause unnecessary head wear.

THE SUBSTRATE

The base material that the coating coats, the material that gives the disk its physical shape, is termed its *substrate*. Many of the disk specifications relate to the nature of that substrate material. One set of media specifications dictates the tensile strength of the media and its coefficients of expansion. The substrate's tensile strength will guarantee a disk that won't stretch too easily; the coefficients of expansion dictate what will happen to the shape of the tracks on the disk as the disk warms up or cools down.

Disks—especially floppies—tend to expand unevenly, distorting the tracks you've written on them into an ovoid shape. If the tracks distort too much from their original shape, a head positioned by a stepper motor stands no chance of being able to accurately track the new shape. Some of the time it will be on the track and some of the time it won't. It will lose the data you've recorded.

This particular specification is intended to be tight enough to allow a stepper motor-positioned head to track the normal expansion and contraction that a floppy will experience throughout its rated temperature (4 to 50°C). But other standards will furnish their own requirements. As a rule of thumb, the biaxially oriented polyethylene terephthalate film used as a substrate for most floppies (and specified by the X3.82-1980 spec) will require the use of tracking servos whenever you want tracking densities to exceed 4 tracks/mm.

Besides expansion and contraction, you have to worry about stretching. It isn't always temperature that is the culprit. Mechanical forces within the drive or poor handling outside of it can also make it go out of round. The disk's resistance to stretching is its *tensile strength*. The tensile strength specification puts things in terms of a *tensile yield force*. This is the force required to elongate the sample by 3 percent. For ANSI's 5.25-in. floppy specification, the tensile yield force must be at least 14 pounds-force.

Tear resistance is measured too. It's no good to have a disk that tears instead of stretching. You still lose information when there is mechanical stress. Using a test that measures the Elmendorf tear strength, the standard calls out a minimum of 1.89 ounces-force as measured using the American National Standard Method of Test for Propagation Tear Resistance of Plastic Film and Thin Sheeting (ANSI/ASTM D 1922–67).

These sets of specifications certainly limit the possible material choices for floppy disk media, but the specification falls far short of dictating one. This leaves room for media manufacturers to experiment with coatings that will work with the present generation of drives, yet provide the performance that will be needed by the higher storage capacities of the next generation.

RIGID MEDIA

For high-capacity data storage most drive manufacturers turn to the rigid disk. Because the rigidity of the substrate makes it much more stable than a floppy, the rigid disk can achieve higher capacities by, among other things, flying the heads closer to the disk surface.

But all is not roses. Rigid disks have different problems and different construction than floppies. The standard oxide-coated disk consists of an aluminum substrate coated with a slurry (a thin, watery mixture) of basically the same iron-oxide particles used in floppy diskettes. The result is a disk that looks like the 5.25-in. media shown in Figure 3–5.

Courtesy of Charlton Associates Inc.

FIGURE 3–5
A 5.25-in. rigid disk.

There will be a tremendous variation in disk products simply because of the variations in raw materials and processing. Aluminum for the substrate, for example, comes in many qualities, and disk vendors must work closely with the suppliers to find aluminum which will stamp out smoothly and minimize the amount of burnishing needed to turn an aluminum cutout into a disk substrate.

And the quality of coating and lubricants depends on the quality of their basic ingredients as well. Media manufacturers employ a fair number of chemists who constantly search for ways to make subtle changes in the specific formulae that make the media more reliable, easier to produce, or just plain better.

Manufacturing a rigid disk is a complex process that requires 13 to 15 tightly controlled manufacturing steps. The exact number of steps depends on the manufacturer. Charlton Associates Inc., for example, takes its product through the process outlined in Figure 3–6. The first six steps ensure that the process produces a substrate worth coating; the next three apply the oxide coating; and the last four take care of the final preparation. The steps labeled F1 and F2 refer to a

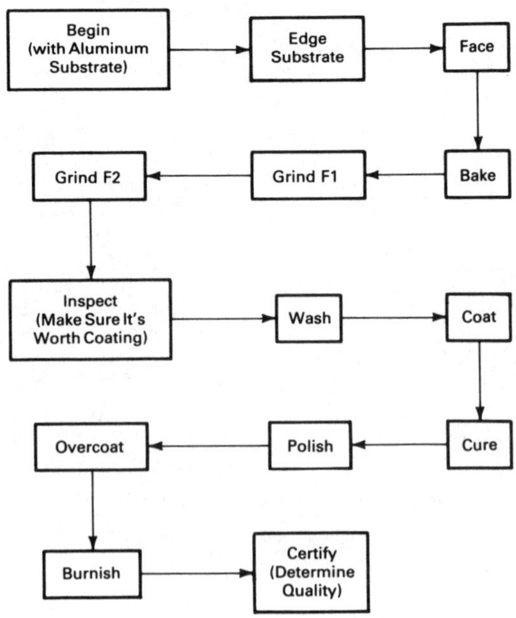

FIGURE 3–6
A typical rigid disk manufacturing process.

two-step grinding process that takes the surface to a coarse finish (F1) and then a fine finish (F2).

After applying the coating and curing it, there's yet another grinding process—polishing. The coating on a Winchester rigid disk is ground down to a thickness of approximately 40 microns. After polishing, it is lubricated with a waxlike substance and the surface is burnished.

Properly applied, the lubricant's job is to allow the Winchester heads to land and take off from the disk surface, and it also serves to protect the disk surface from inadvertant contact with the heads at other times. If it weren't for the lubricant, the heads would remove part of the oxide coating every time they landed, or in the case of plated media, the heads might even fuse to the media. If the lubricant is too thin, it quickly wears off. It if is too thick, however, you still have a problem. When the disk isn't being used, the wax will migrate from the disk surface to the heads, creating a buildup that will hold the heads prisoner when you try to spin the disk.

A second type of rigid disk media used in high-capacity storage is plated media. The idea behind this media is that a magnetic metallic coating will have better (and more easily controlled) magnetic properties than one made of magnetic particles diffused in a binder. And the disk's smoothness can be more readily guaranteed through the plating process than by burnishing an oxide coating.

The first plated disks were manufactured with fairly thick layers of the metallic coating. These are the thick-film disks. But, because the thickness of the magnetic coatings is one of the factors that determines the disk's maximum storage capacity, the trend is toward thinner and thinner coatings. The thicker the coating, the more the magnetic domains tend to spread out. The thinner the coating, therefore, the higher the possible bit densities. In fact, there is almost an inverse relationship between the spacing of flux transitions on the disk and the coating thickness. Thus, we see the birth of so-called thin-film media. This type of media uses a 5-micron thick metallic layer that is plated on the substrate. Oxide coatings simply won't go on that thinly.

This makes it the thinnest coating of all the technologies we've examined. The film is so thin that small variations in the fabrication process can result in wildly varying magnetic characteristics from disk to disk. To standardize the process satisfactorily, manufacturers have turned to semiconductor technologies. The metallic alloys are deposited by rigidly controlled evaporation, electrodeposition, or sputtering techniques.

This thin metallic film has a higher coercive force than iron oxide does. The actual coercive force that a particular disk has depends on four major factors:

- The film's thickness
- The film's composition
- The deposition parameters
- The annealing process

If the drive then uses a read/write head with a high magnetic energy level, it can write with sharp transitions between magnetic domains. Thus, the thin-film disk can support higher flux densities than can oxide-coated disks. Furthermore, the thinner coating means that saturation recording can take place with a smaller induced field than it can with particulate (oxide) media.

Proponents of the plated media are also quick to point out that its relative smoothness, compared to oxide-coated disks, means that the repeated takeoffs and landings of the heads won't produce additional debris inside the sealed assembly the way oxide-coated disks have been known to do. When manufacturers first tried to use plated media, however, a problem quickly showed up. When the ultrasmooth metal surface of the heads met the smooth metal surface of the disk, the two bonded together. When the drive started up again, the head was often torn from the head assembly. To offset this problem, both the head and disk are coated with lubricants.

SMOOTH SAILING

Because the heads fly so low over a Winchester disk, it's imperative that the disk surface be inherently smooth as well as clean. The smallest surface defect (asperity) can prove fatal to a head that is passing only 0.4 μm over the disk's surface, as the IBM® 3370 does.* To ensure the smoothness of the disk, manufacturers such as IBM check every disk with a defect-spotting technique known as a glide test.

The glide test entails mounting a piezoelectric crystal on a special head slider as shown in Figure 3–7. The test engineer then increases the slider's tip mass, making the entire slider assembly fly closer to the surface than a conventional head does. Any unacceptably large defect will touch the slider putting pressure on the crystal and thus producing a voltage output from the crystal.

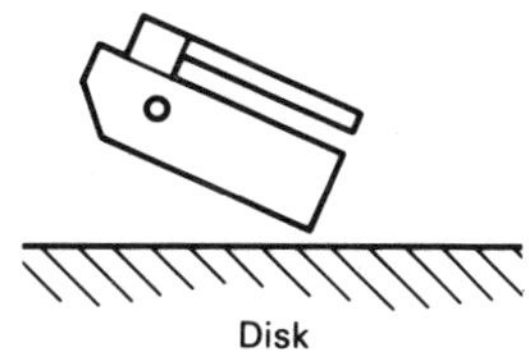

FIGURE 3–7
A piezoelectric crystal mounted on a head slider determines if the disk surface is smooth enough for low-flying Winchester heads.

By reading a record of the crystal's output voltages from a strip recorder, a technician gets a detailed map of the precise location of defects and their relative size. This record can become part of the disk's permanent file, helping designers track down problems that might crop up later in the drive's lifetime.

And even a well-made disk can suffer from defects. Most platters have one somewhere. Manufacturers control their products carefully, however. If you look at the defect record that comes with nearly every fixed disk, you'll see that there are fewer than three defects, typically.

Not all defects come from irregularities in the materials or process. Handling can damage a disk just as easily. But, when there are particulate contaminations or coating debris accumulations, the problems must be corrected. By detecting these defects early on, a manufacturer can catch potentially bad batches of disks that result when the process isn't working exactly right.

The glide test gives the drive and media makers a better idea of the nature of the disk's surface than simple measurements of the surface roughness do because it works exactly the same way the head will when the disk is actually in use. It is an objective measurement of the disk's performance at working speeds and under realistic conditions.

---

*IBM is a registered trademark of International Business Machines Corporation.

INTERFACING TO THE SYSTEM II

4 Data on the Disk

Up to this point we've discussed the methods of physically storing data on the disk—the magnetization of the oxide particles in the disk's coating—and the way that the disk positions heads and turns the spindle. These two areas should give you a solid grasp of what is going on inside the peripheral. But that isn't enough.

A disk drive is much more than an interesting technological device; it is a vital system component. As such, it must work with the other system components toward some purpose, or else it is worthless. So, you must also learn some of the techniques and technologies that usually fall under the heading *system integration.* You must learn how to get the most out of the drive that you choose to use.

To adequately address this aspect of the drive's existence, it's important to view the process of integrating the drive into the system in two separate dimensions: We must see its interface to the system as an interactive part of the complete system operation; we must also consider the drive's physical interface to the system.

The first view, that of the drive as an interactive system component, is almost as much a philosophical problem as anything else; the second view, however, gets back to basic electronics and deals with the specific electronic connections between a disk drive and the host computer.

In this chapter we will address the ways in which data is stored on the disk. This encompasses two tangential ideas—the logical arrangement of data on the disk surface and the recording scheme used to put it there. The logical arrangement takes into account the way the system treats data and programs. Under this heading we examine the various logical groupings of data. The recording scheme tells you a little more about storage technology itself and defines the limits (maximum storage capacity) of a particular technology. You'll need to understand both to make much sense of rotating media.

THE REASON FOR BEING

The proper discussion of the disk as a system component begins with a description of its complete function. What does a disk drive do for the system? Why bother to have a disk at all? Why not just add enough semiconductor memory to hold all of the data and programs?

Simply speaking, the primary function of a disk drive is to provide nonvolatile storage of data and programs. In this context *nonvolatile* means that, under normal conditions, you don't lose the information when you turn the power off. Most random access memory is volatile. You can't use volatile memory for long-term storage of anything. The disk gives you a reasonable way of storing data for a long period of time.

Secondly, the computer can only address a certain amount of memory directly. An 8-bit computer, for example, can address only 64K bytes of main memory. The limitation is a function of the number of address lines. Any processor can address 2^N bytes of memory, where N is the number of address lines. Any memory over that amount requires special addressing schemes, such as configuring the memory into switchable banks, to make it accessible to the computer. While that constraint doesn't keep designers from adding memory beyond 64K to 8-bit machines, it does mean that disk drives are a more practical, and cost-effective, solution in most cases.

A disk drive is useful, therefore, because it gives the system large amounts of easily accessible, nonvolatile storage capacity in a compact package. And the memory is, in one sense at least, directly addressable. The processor makes all of its requests by file name.

The host computer normally executes (runs) programs that are stored in a known location in its main memory and operates on data that is also stored in main memory. It never actually uses data that is still stored only on the disk. It must read the data into memory first. To make the information stored on a disk easily accessible, therefore, we have to do a bit of planning.

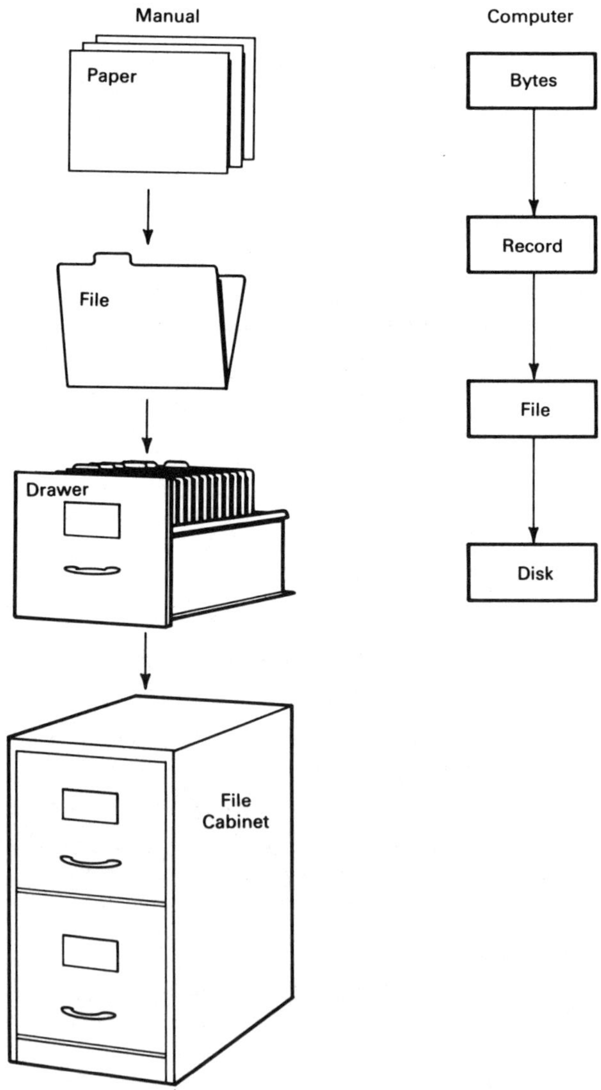

FIGURE 4–1
Think of the disk storage as you would a filing cabinet.

The proper integration of the disk into the system will involve a logical hardware-software construction that ensures a smooth flow of data between memory and the disk, plus a consistent scheme of indexing information that will allow the system to find exactly the data or program that it needs quickly. This indexing problem will become clearer once you understand the disk's role a bit better.

The disk acts as little more than a file cabinet for the computer. The data and programs that go into it must be available as needed. The filing system, therefore, must meet the needs of the overall system design.

SIMPLE FILING

When you file information away in a file cabinet, you want to be sure that you can retrieve it easily at some later date. The same applies to disk storage. A computer system needs to have a method of storing and retrieving data that is fairly simple and reliable. There's no advantage to a system that makes offline storage too complex. A complicated system would require more space to store the records than it would to store the data. And a cumbersome electronic system is no better than an efficient manual system.

The disk's organization describes the orderly placement of data; it corresponds to the rudiments of a filing system. In a manual system you put words on paper, paper in files, files in drawers, and drawers in cabinets. Although the disk has no physical drawers or sheets of paper, it does have files. The files, in turn, have sections called *records*. The records are the objects that the file consists of. In a database, for example, a record could represent one customer.

With a little effort you can arrange a disk's organization such that it exhibits the electronic equivalent of sheets of paper and drawers. Each unit of information—data or program, the computer doesn't care which—is stored as a separate file. No good analogy is without some toehold in reality. Thus, you, as the user, get to decide what information goes into what files. The comparison of the manual and computerized systems won't necessarily be exactly as the chart shown in Figure 4–1 portrays it, but this example will help you visualize the disk storage techniques.

Although both the recording format and the disk organization directly affect the precise placement of bits on the disk's surface, for the moment we only want to address the organization of data. This organization is a logical arrangement, as you'll see, more than it is a physical one. Understanding it requires that we deal with the abstract concept of a file rather than the physics of magnetic recording.

Of course, this entire analogy is just a convenience. The computer system doesn't work the same way that we do at all. But, to make our use of a computer system a straightforward task, the system designer will have to create a *file structure,* probably in the operating system.

The file structure is nothing more than a set of rules that describes the procedures for handling blocks of data. The rules define how large the records are, how they are addressed within the file, and so on.

These file-manipulation procedures are for the computer's direction, not the operator's. Among other things the file structure will define some special characters that it will use to indicate such parameters as the end of a file (EOF).

Along with the file structure goes some file-addressing information (FAI). This information acts as an index that can direct our file-oriented requests to specific tracks and sectors on the disk surface.

Consider a practical example of this. You are building a database of disk drive manufacturers. This database is a file. In the file you are creating a separate record for each manufacturer, containing the firm's name, address, telephone number, and the name of an individual in marketing. The record contains these entries. When you want to update the information, how do you retrieve a particular record? The answer is that a file can be structured in three basic ways. The files can be constructed such that the records can be read

- Sequentially
- Directly
- Indirectly

Let's see what this means. Sequential files are a very efficient means of storing information, but extremely awkward for use in database management. The idea is that a file becomes nothing more than all of its records in sequential order. The only file-addressing information that the system keeps track of is the location of the file on the disk. Although the disk itself is a random access device, it has no idea of where the individual records are located on its surface.

To find a particular record, therefore, you must read through the entire file until you come to it. Every time that you want any information from a file, the system must read the entire file from the disk; every time any record is changed, the computer must write the entire file back to the disk. Referring back to our filing system analogy for a moment, this is akin to being able to locate a particular letter, but having to read it from beginning to end in order to locate a particular bit of information.

Direct access files allow you to go directly to any desired record within the file. There are a number of ways that a system designer can use to implement this strategy, but the important thing is that when you ask for the third record of a particular file, the system can locate that record's address directly. Now you can change a single record, say a customer address, without reading through the entire customer file.

The difficulty with this type of record keeping is that each record must be the same size—the size of the largest record you'll ever need. Thus, managing your data wastes a fair amount of valuable disk space. Imagine having to allocate records large enough for the longest customer names you'll encounter (including Aloisious Ambercrombie III), and then most of your customers having names like Ed Teja. The trade-off implicit in this technique is that space (disk space) is less important than getting the fastest possible access to your information.

Indirect access files have a mechanism that eventually leads you to a particular record within a file, but you don't get at the record directly. Some preliminary sequential steps lead the algorithm to the address of the record. There are any number of techniques of referencing the computer to the record it wants.

You might put a table of record addresses at the beginning of a file, for example, and then, after the file is read into memory, be able to access the desired record by looking up its address in the table. You indirectly access the address. Such a scheme lets you use variable-length records, and, although it is slower than direct access, indirect access is faster than sequential access. There are trade-offs everywhere.

RECORDING METHODS

But how is the data actually stored on the disk? The most obvious retort is that it is done magnetically. That is the physicist's answer. But what is the engineer's answer? Beyond the physics of recording lie the methods of recording. There are two aspects to the job of storing data on the disk: organizing the disk surface into logical units and coding, or the recording scheme, which stores the data on the surface.

The recording scheme is the code that you use to convert digital 1s and 0s into flux reversals. It determines how many magnetic domains it takes to store a bit of information. The recording scheme depends on the requirements of the disk controller and deals with the technology of retrieving individual data bits. It answers the following questions: How do you tell data on the disk from anything else? How do you translate magnetic patterns into data? What coding scheme allows us to put data on the disk?

The earliest coding scheme used for storing data on disk was frequency modulation (FM). Most of the single-density floppy drives are still encoded with FM. It is a reliable and simple scheme. The term *single density* is a relative term, of course. It only became single density when manufacturers introduced more efficient coding schemes that offered higher recording densities.

In an FM-coded system the smallest division of information on the disk is not a bit, but a 4-μsec-long *bit cell*. Each bit cell contains one bit of information (a data bit) and a timing, or clock, pulse. It works like this. At the beginning of every bit cell you'll find a flux reversal. If the logic level was *low,* at the beginning of the next bit cell, the logic level goes *high*. If the logic level was *high,* it goes *low*. Thus, we say that we have marked the beginning of the bit cell.

This marker is the *clock pulse*. It always takes up exactly one-half of the bit cell. The second half of the bit cell contains the data—it tells us the logic level of the bit itself. A flux reversal indicates a 1 and no change indicates a 0. These concepts define what within the bit cell constitutes a logical 1 or 0. Figure 4–2 illustrates some sample bit cells to give you a better idea of how the scheme works in practice. It's always easier to visualize the various encoding schemes when you can see what the bit cell logic looks like.

The idea behind FM coding is quite simple. In reading a disk, whenever the read/write electronics encounter a flux reversal, it can simply read through a few reversals until two halves of a bit cell pass by the heads, where there are no flux changes. We will instantly know that this is a 0. In a bit cell that contains a 1 you'll always see a flux reversal, and the cell always starts with a reversal, so any space 1 bit cell long with no changes has to be a 0. Simple.

As we mentioned, FM coding is reliable. The only problem with it is that it can't store data densely. The basic inefficiency of FM coding is that it takes the space of two flux reversals, or 1 bit cell, to indicate the value of each bit. The bit cell is an awkward way of encoding the data. You wind up losing half of the disk's available surface to the clock pulses. This might prove a reliable way to store data, but it is also extremely wasteful.

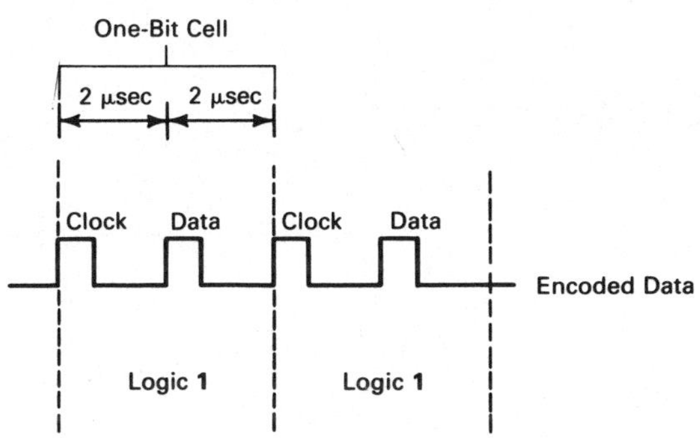

FIGURE 4–2
Sample bit cells.

To get more productive use of the space on the disk, manufacturers began to look for ways to eliminate at least some of the clock pulses. Clock pulses, like the servo data we talked about earlier, eat up disk space that could be better used for increasing the disk's storage capacity without having to improve the recording technology. This is the best kind of capacity increase. When the storage capacity is already there, and you just have to use it more efficiently, you don't have to worry about breaking in a new hardware design.

The search for more efficient techniques produced a modified FM (MFM) coding scheme. The modification of the scheme was to make the data self-clocking—eliminating the need for clock pulses per se. Let's see how that works out.

On an MFM-coded disk, each bit cell contains a single pulse. Right off the bat this lets us reduce the size of a bit cell from the 4 μsec required by FM encoding to 2 μsec. All data bits are written in the middle of the bit cell. So, if there's a transition in the middle of the cell, it represents a logic 1; if there's no transition in the middle of the cell, it represents a logic 0.

Ordinarily, when the disk is writing a series of 0s (no transition), it will mark the beginning of each bit cell with a clock pulse for timing purposes. When the 0 follows a 1, however, it leaves the clock pulse out. Thus, most of the clock pulses are eliminated, saving a great deal of disk space for data. In order to visualize this encoding scheme properly, take a good look at Figure 4–3. It contrasts a series of FM-encoded data with MFM encoding.

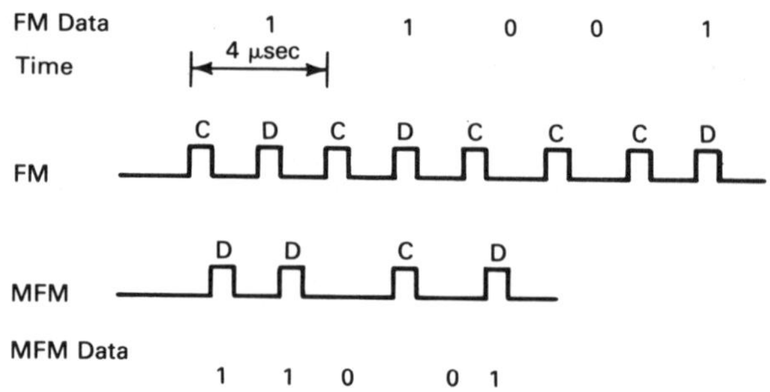

FIGURE 4–3
MFM saves disk space when compared to FM.

Modified MFM (or M^2FM) reduces the number of clock pulses even further than MFM. This time the clock pulses that would ordinarily be associated with a logic 0 which is preceded by a 0 are eliminated. The fourth 0 in any series, however, is still clocked. It is another incremental change that improves storage efficiencies.

SEPARATING DATA FROM CLOCK

In order to use the data stored on the disk in the host computer, you not only have to get it from the disk, you must also separate it from the clock pulses. These were put on the disk to help the drive locate the data in the first place, you'll recall, and have no meaning whatsoever to the host computer. In an FM-coded system, this is a relatively easy task. Once you find the beginning of a bit cell, you know exactly where the data will be located—and the clock pulse clearly marks the beginning of the bit cell. You know how long the bit cell is (4 μsec), and you have a flux reversal to keep the timing on track—synchronizing the clocks. It's like closing your eyes during the clock portion of the cell. To decode the information, just establish a 2-μsec window centered around the center of the bit cell—beginning about 1 μsec after the clock pulse.

Decoding data in an MFM system requires that the data separator watch two windows in the data patterns: the first 1-μsec window tests for the presence of clock pulses at the leading edge of the bit cell; the second 1-μsec window tests for data bits. You can't time the data window from the clock pulse this time because there won't always be one handy. This means that you must constantly be measuring from the last pulse that you did see, trying to center the window around the pulse.

Unfortunately, a 1-μsec window doesn't always allow enough space to accommodate for the amount of bit shifting you're likely to see in floppy disk drives. To account for this problem, most data separators designed for double-density recording have specially designed bit-shift compensation circuitry. This compensation technique bears closer inspection.

First, let's look at exactly what is happening. This shift-

FIGURE 4–4
The waveform readback from the disk is more bell shaped than the square wave you recorded.

ing of the data pulse's position within the bit cell, termed *peak shifting,* is caused by interference in between pulses that you are reading. Although the pulses are distinct square waves in our representations, when the drive reads them from the disk, the readback waveform tends to look more like the bell-shaped curve shown in Figure 4–4.

When the drive reads tightly packed data (or data and clock) pulses, regardless of the encoding scheme, there can be some overlap in the signals. The read amplifier doesn't know the difference between two overlapped signals (as shown in Figure 4–5a) and a single sine wave (Figure 4–5b). The analog circuitry just looks at the total value of the signal. Thus, to the read channel, the peaks appear to have shifted from their original positions.

One popular method of compensating for this peak shift is to actually put the flux reversals on the disk in positions that will move the peaks back to where they belong. This is called *write compensation,* because the drive compensates for the peak shift when it writes the data rather than when it reads it.

DESIGNING IT IN

If you put the data separator in the disk drive, the controller will pass simple NRZ (nonreturn to zero) data to the drive. This scheme is perhaps the simplest of all codes. A 1 followed by a 0 produces a flux change; so does a 0 followed by a 1. In other words a high logic level is a 1 and a low logic level is a 0. Clock pulses are eliminated completely.

This arrangement of the components makes whatever encoding scheme the drive uses totally transparent to the controller, as well as to the host computer. That is an advantage for the system, and for you as the system integrator, because it allows the same controller to work equally well for a variety of drives using unique encoding schemes. Using run-length limited codes (self-clocking coding schemes), these drives can achieve the maximum use of the

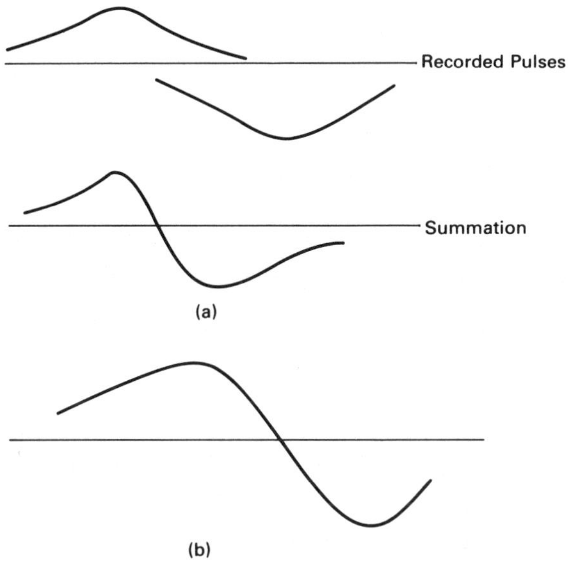

FIGURE 4–5
The readback circuitry can't differentiate between (a) two overlapped signals and (b) a single sine wave.

disk space available. Run-length limited codes can provide some data compression, which in turn reduces the amount of data the controller must send to the disk to store a particular quantity of information.

This is the attitude taken by the manufacturers who have proposed both the enhanced small disk interface (ESDI) and the adoption of the ANSI interface standard for high-capacity Winchester disk drives. These drives can take advantage of run-length limited codes, specifically fixed-length codes, to squeeze every possible bit of data onto the disk. Yet, the controller doesn't have to deal with the encoding scheme. It sees only NRZ data, just as it would from any other peripheral. This not only simplifies controller designs, it makes the software necessary to drive the disk easier to write as well.

While relocating the data separator from the controller board into the disk drive itself can provide some dramatic improvements in controller throughput, it doesn't change the recording scheme that the disk uses. Still, the newer disk designs will have added intelligence within the drive, and that will mean that you can expect almost all future drives to accept NRZ-coded data, regardless of their individual recording scheme.

5 Formatters

Chapter 4 left a gap in its discussion of organizing data on the disk. We've seen the logical organization, and we've examined the recording schemes, but we haven't established how a drive will know where to find data on the disk. At what point on the disk does the drive start reading bit cells? Does every bit cell contain data? These questions are found in the structure of the disk's data *format.*

There is a method to the madness of representing data as groups of 1s and 0s arranged on a disk surface—a method that allows the system to quickly locate any specific piece of information it might need. But, this method requires more structure than just the *logical* organization we encountered in the last chapter. It takes a specific *physical* organization. More precisely, this method is known as the disk's *data format.* And there are several possible data formats that a disk designer (usually) or system integrator (sometimes) can choose from.

A data format is actually nothing more than a formula or strategy for arranging the data (or anything else for that matter) on the disk's surface. (For the purposes of this chapter, anything stored on a disk will be referred to as data, whether it is actually data or a program.) The current formulae, while not completely arbitrary, is always going to be something that works, rather than necessarily an optimum strategy.

ORGANIZING THE TRACKS

You already know that the data is arranged in concentric rings, termed *tracks,* around the disk, but until now we have not delved any deeper than that into the structure. But data doesn't come neatly packaged in track-length pieces. It comes as bytes or even bits. But how is a particular bit on that track labeled or identified? It isn't. Instead, the system views each track as being divided into blocks. The number of blocks can vary from system to system, as can their size. In each particular format the blocks will have a specific size, measured in terms of bytes. Thus, the physical size will depend on the encoding technique and vary from disk drive to disk drive. Each of these blocks is termed a *sector*.

Most of the computer's data is *byte oriented*. That means that the computer deals with the information 8 bits, or 1 byte, at a time. The disk is organized in the same way. Thus, it is enough to know that you are interested in, for example, the third byte in sector two of track 44. This might be the address of the beginning of a particular record within a file, for example. With the ability to locate information that specifically, the computer can quickly retrieve any information that it might need.

The first floppy disk, used in the IBM System 370 computer, had a format that divided each track of the 8-in. diskette into 26 sectors. Each sector was 128 bytes long. So each track could hold 3328 bytes (or 26,624 bits) of data. A 77-track, single-sided disk holds 256,256 bytes (256K) of data.

You don't actually have access to that much storage space, however. Track 00 is reserved for Data Set Labels, which identify the type of information found on the other tracks. Tracks 74 and 75 are held in reserve, to be used if other tracks become flawed. This reduces the disk's actual capacity to 246,272 bytes, but it is still referred to as a 256K-byte format.

The actual amount of data that can be stored on the diskette is called the *formatted* storage capacity, as opposed to *unformatted* storage. The unformatted storage capacity is the maximum number of flux changes that the drive could store at the track density; the formatted storage is the amount of organized data that you can put on the diskette.

Regardless of the specific recording format the disk drive uses, there will always be some difference between all of the space available on the disk—its unformatted capacity—and the usable space—its formatted capacity. The difference between the two figures represents the disk space that must be used to store location, identification, and timing information on the disk in order to let the system know at all times which track and sector it is reading. This is the storage *overhead,* and you'll learn more about the overhead information as we go along.

Consider the format of Seagate Technology's ST506 5.25-in. Winchester disk drive. This is the format we will use to discuss the various components of the format. This format is not necessarily the best, but it illustrates the form and function of a typical organization method.

The ST506's unformatted storage capacity is 6.38M bytes; after the manufacturer formats the disk, it can store 5M bytes. Where does the extra capacity go? It's used up in providing information for the drive's operation. Let's take a close look.

Seagate Technology chose to format data on the disk in a slightly modified version of the IBM System 34 double-density format—the same one used on many floppy disks. Each of the ST506's tracks is formatted into 32 sectors; each sector is 256 bytes long. This formatting gives each track 8192 bytes of data storage.

But the drive itself can do better than this format implies. Its particular encoding scheme (a double-density scheme termed modified frequency modulation, or MFM) is efficient enough to give each track a nominal capacity of 10,416 bytes. This means that, if you multiply the storage density (bits/in.) of each track times the length of the track, you'd find space enough for 10,416 bytes, or 83,328 bits. But 2224 bytes on every track are lost when the disk is formatted. Although each sector is really 314 bytes long, you can only use 256 bytes for data storage. That means that each sector has 58 bytes of overhead. But every byte seemingly lost serves a purpose, as you will see.

The reason that so much data storage capacity gets lost is that the drive needs a great deal of information to do its job. Let's take a look at the ST506's sector format and see how that works out.

THE SECTOR LAYOUT

The sector is the smallest unit of data on the disk. Every track is divided up into some number of sectors. Each sector consists of three standard component parts: the identification field, the data field, and the gaps. The sector needs an identification field to let the drive know which sector is which.

Disks can be either soft or hard sectored. A hard-sectored disk has a physical indication of where the beginning of the disk is. Typically, it is a hole. The drive will shine a light at the disk, and when an optical sensor on the other side of the diskette detects light, the drive knows that the index hole has passed by. A floppy diskette that is hard sectored will usually have either 10 or 16 sectors per track.

The Seagate disk, like most rigid disks and many floppies, is soft sectored. This means that there is no physical clue, no hardware indication, of where any sector begins or ends. In order for the drive to know where a sector begins, and what sector is beginning, therefore, each sector begins with an identification (ID) field. This field contains the physical sector address and the cylinder and head information. This is also where you'll find the defect flag that warns the system if the sector it is about to read contains a permanent defect or is considered marginal for data recording—it indicates one of the so-called hard errors. (Seagate limits any drive to fewer than three hard errors per disk, or eight errors per drive. The first cylinder, cylinder 0, must always be error-free on all drives, however. This is where the directory information is stored.) A logical 1 in position seven of the ID field's head byte indicates the presence of a defect.

FINDING THE ID FIELD

But how does the system even know that it is reading an ID field? What distinguishes ID information from data? A simple data pattern. Once the head has stepped to the proper track, it starts reading immediately. Every field, whether an ID field or a data field, is indicated by a unique character, the 2-byte *address mark*. An A1 is the alert signal. If the address mark consists of an A1 followed by an FE, the drive knows that the next thing it will see is an ID field. If the address mark is an A1 followed by an F8, the drive knows that the very next byte it will see begins a data field. The first 2 bytes of an ID field, therefore, contain the hexadecimal characters A1FE.

All the drive needs to do, therefore, is a bit of pattern matching. It looks for the proper data pattern, indicating that it has found an address mark. Once the first ID field has been located, the drive has a relatively easy time locating everything else.

CHECKING ERRORS

In addition to the location and defect information it provides, the ID field has, as its last character, a 16-bit cyclic redundancy check (CRC) character that the system uses to detect mistakes in reading the ID field. CRC checks are the most common way of ensuring the system's data integrity.

This cyclic redundancy code is a linear code, usually a polynomial. The disk controller circuitry will divide the data it writes to the disk by this polynomial and then store the result of its computation as the CRC character.

When the system reads data back from the disk, it performs the computation again (on the data it reads from the disk) and compares the result to the result stored on the disk. If the results don't match, the system can try reading

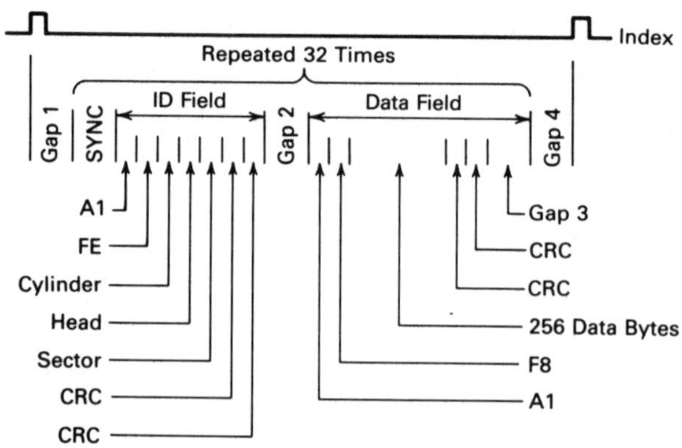

Courtesy of Seagate Technology.

FIGURE 5–1
The ST506 track format provides gaps which accommodate fluctuations in the disk's rotation speed.

the data again. Unless the data on the disk is actually corrupted, this procedure will ensure data integrity. Even the simplest polynomial should detect all single-bit errors.

In larger, more sophisticated, systems the use of complex error-correcting formulae can ensure that data integrity to an amazing degree. Not only do these systems use more extensive error checking, but they even supply a certain amount of error correction, based on the computational results.

FINDING THE DATA

Following the ID field is the sought-after data field. Here is where the data is actually stored. But even the data field isn't *all* data. The first part of the data field provides its 2-byte address mark (A1F8). Then you get 256 bytes of actual data, followed by a 16-bit (2-byte) CRC character that the system can use to make sure that it read its data properly. So the data field itself has to be 260 bytes long in order to provide 256 bytes of storage.

IT'S ALL IN THE TIMING

Reading (and writing) involves proper timing. You can't just write data anywhere in a track—you must write in a specified area of a sector. Having fixed-length data fields helps a great deal, but you can't count on even a fixed-length field always taking up the same amount of space on the disk surface. The words *fixed length* give you a false sense of security. The length is fixed only in terms of the amount of information it stores, not necessarily in terms of the amount of physical space it uses.

Whenever you try to read and write data on any electromechanical device, there are going to be some physical variations that must be overcome. The mechanical nature of the device means that there will be some irregularities in its components, causing variations in the mechanical motions of the device and problems in timing. No bearing is perfectly round, or smooth, after all. The system can accommodate these variations, at least to some extent, through the prudent use of flexible space fillers called *gaps*.

As the sector layout illustrates (Figure 5–1), the Seagate format has four gaps surrounding the data and ID fields.

Each gap has a particular function, and all of the gaps act together to furnish the system with the fine tuning it requires for its physical and timing relationships. Each gap serves a unique purpose: Together they equalize the mechanical irregularities.

Three of these gaps recur in every sector; the other two, gaps 1 and 4 are found once on each track.

Gap 1 ranges in size from 12 to 16 bytes, in order to accommodate variations in index detection. Seagate Technology ships the drive with this gap set to 16 bytes. The gap follows the index mark and gives the drive a chance to react to it.

Gap 2 follows the ID field, filling in all of the space between the CRC bytes of the ID field and the data field's address mark. This 16-byte gap gives the drive a chance to synchronize its write amplitude. It uses this space to practice writing until it "locks up" the phase-lock loop in the host computer's data separator electronics. It acts as a scratch pad for the drive to practice writing until it gets it right.

Gap 3 allows for those small, but inevitable, variations in the drive's spindle speed. There's no way to guarantee that the spindle will always turn at exactly the same rate; any changes in its speed will affect how much disk space a given amount of data takes, and, therefore, it can alter the physical length of a field.

Assume, for example, that you are updating a sector, and that the disk is now running faster than when you originally wrote the sector. When you rewrite the sector, the disk will be writing at a fixed rate, but the disk is running faster. More of the disk will pass under the heads during any given time interval. The transfer of data to the disk is gated by time, however. As a result, you are now spreading the data over a larger (longer) space on the disk than it originally occupied. You are in danger of overwriting the sector that follows this one.

An 8-byte gap placed here when the disk is formatted will give you enough room to store the data in 256-byte sectors without overwriting anything as long as the spindle speed variation is within 3 percent of its nominal speed

(3600 rpm). Greater fluctuations will, of course, still cause trouble, but the disk is manufactured to stay well within the 3 percent margin. Most rigid disks are specified to remain within about 1 percent of the stated spindle speed. The 8 bytes, therefore, give you a 300 percent safety margin over the drive specification.

Gap 4 has the same basic function as gap 3, but it buffers speed variations for the entire track, rather than for an individual sector. You don't want to overwrite the beginning of the track. In practice, this gap will be however long it turns out to be when the disk gets formatted, and that, in turn, depends on the spindle speed at that time. By definition, it is all of the space left over. This last gap is sometimes called the *trailing gap*. The only thing that follows the trailing gap is the index mark, and that means that the next revolution of the media has begun.

Notice that there is no servo information included in this format. That should immediately indicate to you that this drive doesn't use an embedded servo. In fact, the ST506 positions its head with a band actuator that is connected to a stepper motor shaft. It is an open-loop system. In a system with an embedded servo, track space would be reserved for the wedges of servo information.

The system component that puts all of the data in the appropriate pattern, or format, is, naturally, the formatter. It is the formatter that bundles the data, performs the CRC checks, and does all of the housekeeping required to keep the disk organized. Simply put, this job boils down to four functions. The formatter must

- Read the formatted data
- Write the formatted data
- Serialize the data
- Deserialize the data

This circuit can be implemented as part of the controller, or it might be a separate component altogether. The decision proves more of a packaging decision than anything else. The trend is toward bundling control and format func-

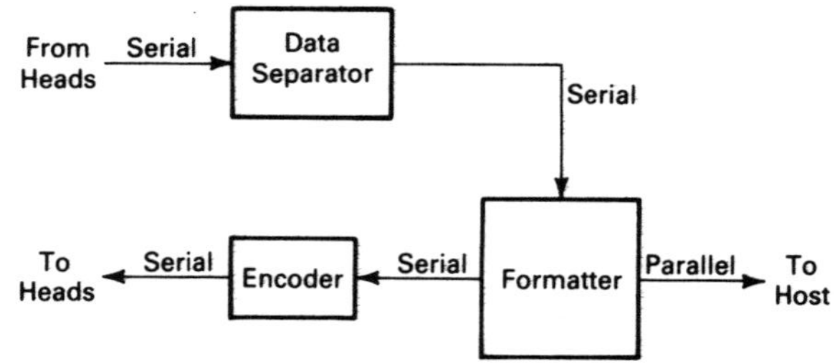

FIGURE 5–2
The formatter processes data, converting the data back and forth from raw parallel data to formatted serial data.

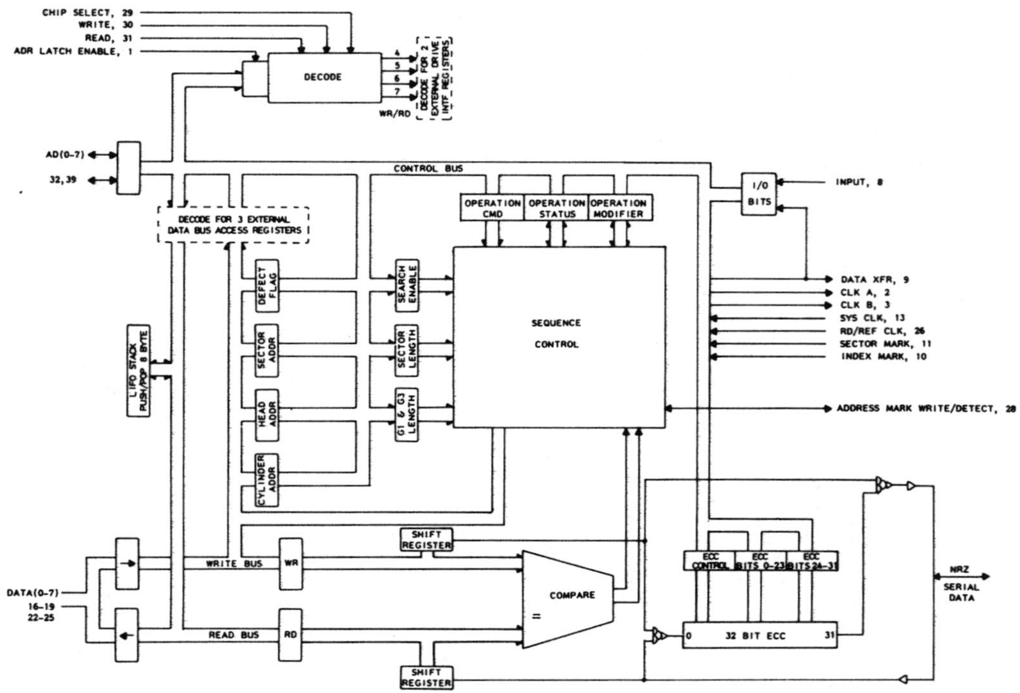

FIGURE 5–3
A Winchester disk controller chip includes the formatter functions.

Courtesy of Adaptec, Inc.

tions together, however. A look at the formatter's function diagram shown in Figure 5-2 illustrates the reason for this trend. While the controller handles all disk operations, the formatter handles most of the data processing. The two are separate parts of one function.

Take, for example, the Winchester Controller Chip (Model AIC-100) from Adaptec shown in the block diagram of Figure 5-3. This chip combines basic controller and format functions. It provides a high-speed search and verify operation that gets you to the track and sector you want quickly. This combines both control and format (read the ID field) capabilities. The chip formats the disk, adding 4 bytes of error-correction data on both the ID and data fields.

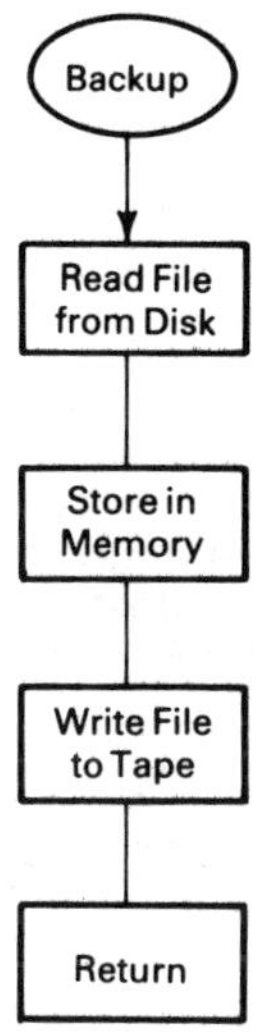

FIGURE 5-4
The flowchart for a typical file backup.

Having a single chip perform both format and control functions makes a great deal of sense. It is a good way to get the maximum potential from your package. And, as disks get smaller, packaging considerations begin to matter more and more.

Combining the formatting and control functions also leads to controllers that can increase system efficiency. Consider the backup problem again. From the controller and formatter point of view, a file backup operation follows the logic shown in the flowchart in Figure 5-4.

The processor gets involved in the process twice for each sector of data backed up. But what if the same controller were to offer a backup command that operated transparently to the host CPU? The flowchart would now appear like the one in Figure 5-5.

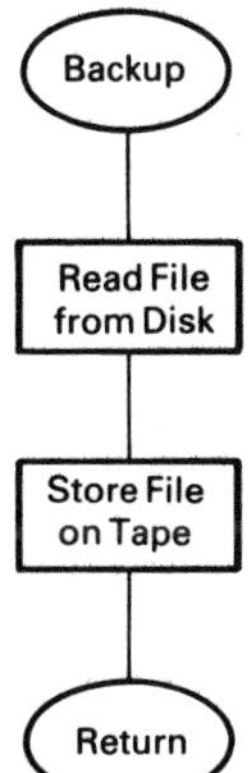

Figure 5-5
Backing up a file with an intelligent controller/formatter.

This approach allows the processor to take care of other system tasks while the disk is being backed up. And there are a number of controllers that offer this feature. Typical of this controller class is the Gypsy Formatter from ADES. The controller connects to the system as shown in Figure 5-6 and can control several memory peripherals. And, when instructed, the controller/formatter does a file backup without the host CPU doing anything but issuing the command. It is totally transparent.

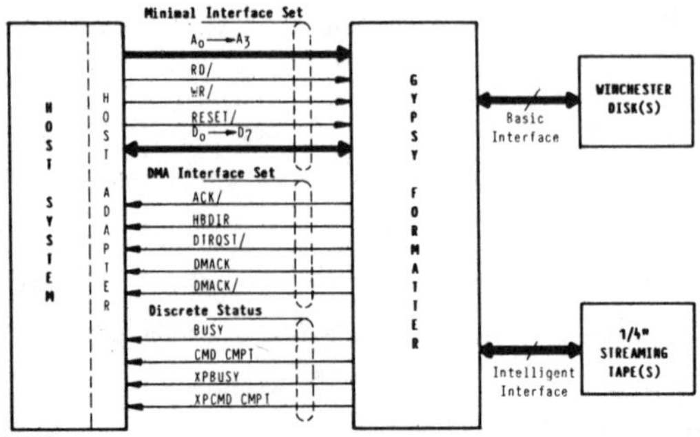

Figure 5–6
A single controller/formatter card can handle multiple devices.

Courtesy of ADES.

SELECTING THE FORMAT

Unfortunately, knowing a typical sector layout doesn't help you select the format you want or need, nor does it tell you anything about the formatters themselves. The chart shown in Figure 5–7 illustrates the many incarnations that a floppy disk can have. For a rigid disk you typically have fewer choices, but you should understand what the format does to you and for you.

The trade-offs you must consider in your selection of a drive are largely price versus capacity. A double-sided drive is more expensive to make than a single-sided unit. And the costs of ownership are higher than the simpler drives, too.

TYPE	PRODUCT DESCRIPTION
8-in. Single-sided Soft-sectored	Single-sided Single-density 128 Bytes
	Single-sided Double-density 256 Bytes
8-in. Single-sided Hard-sectored	Single-sided Single-density 32 Sectors
	Single-sided Double-density 32 sectors
8-in. Double-sided Double-density Soft-sectored	26 Sectors 256 Bytes
	15 Sectors 256 Bytes
	15 Sectors 512 Bytes
	8 Sectors 1024 Bytes
8-in. Double-sided Double-density Hard-sectored	32 Sectors 256 Bytes
5¼-in. Mini Single-sided Single/Double Density	Soft Sectors
	10 Hard Sectors
	16 Hard Sectors
5¼-in. Mini Double-sided Single/Double Density	Soft Sectors
	10 Hard Sectors
	16 Hard Sectors

FIGURE 5–7
Floppy disks come in a variety of formats.

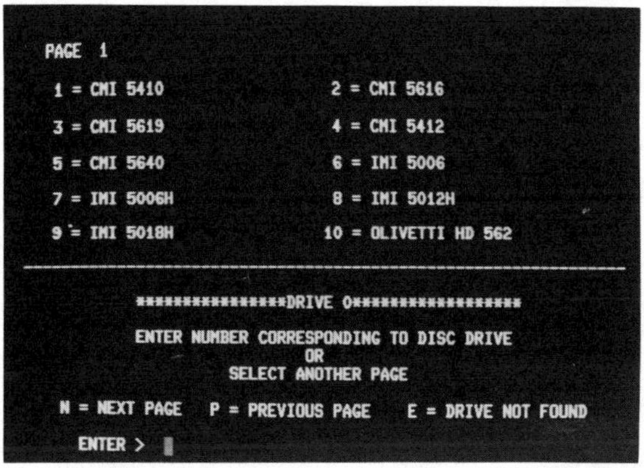

Courtesy of Dilog.

FIGURE 5–8
An interactive formatting program lets you change drives easily without making major changes to system software.

Each disk drive has twice the number of heads to wear out. And the media is marginally more expensive. Double-sided media must be qualified on both sides. More expensive quality control means higher media prices. Double-density recording requires better media and better control over the drive mechanics.

In the end you'll probably have to start with the disk drive that meets your capacity and access time requirements and work backward to the selection of the controller and formatter. The most important consideration is that the disk subsystem as a whole reflect the needs of the computer system rather than a preference for some particular format.

Some manufacturers anticipate the needs of a designer to match the system to a variety of disk formats. Dilog's DQ215 controller/formatter, for example, works with the firm's interactive formatting program to accommodate a variety of 8- and 14-in. Winchester drives from a number of manufacturers.

The menu-driven software package (shown in Figure 5–8) makes changes and reconfigurations simple. You select the number that corresponds to the drive type, and the formatter configures the system to emulate Digital Equipment Corporation's RK06/RK07 drives that the controller is allowing you to replace. In this case the formatting software is concerned with translating the actual format to the one being emulated.

6 Controllers

Thus far, the things we've talked about have either been internal to the drives or closely tied to them. One step removed from the drive, often located physically in the main chassis of the host computer, you'll find a component that can determine whether or not the system and disk drive ever work together well—the controller. The controller's job is to convert the computer's disk access commands into terms that the drive will understand and make sure that the command is satisfactorily carried out.

As its name implies, the controller actually controls the disk drive directly. It directs all of the functions that it takes to accomplish input and output from the disk. It will, for example, issue the step commands that cause the actuator to position the heads over a specific track, check the drive's status, command the spindle to rotate, and enable the read and write heads. It translates a disk access instruction issued by the host computer into the proper series of mechanical directions needed to get the job done.

Because of the controller's role as a system component, it's important that you consider it to be as much a part of the computer system as part of the disk peripheral. Neither fish nor fowl, the controller brings the two system parts together. The controller's physical shape—its board size and format—will most likely be dictated by the computer system's needs, rather than those of the disk drive. Its performance characteristics will be a function of the capabilities and requirements of both the system and the drive. Thus, the decisions you make concerning the controller will be extremely system dependent—that is, they will be based on overall system considerations and characteristics, rather than on reasons that have to do with just the disk drive.

TALKING TO THE COMPUTER

A typical controller provides, in addition to the control circuitry, the circuitry needed to interface the unit to the computer. Thus, the controller furnishes a complete link between the disk drive and the system. Think of the controller's logical position in the system, as illustrated in Figure 6–1. The computer usually has one bus that it uses for transfer of data and commands. (Remember that the one bus has both data and control lines, however.) But the controller has two buses to worry about—one that interconnects to the device and another that interconnects to the host. Over the host bus the controller receives and acknowledges high-level commands from the host computer and transfers processed data to and from the disk. Over the device bus the controller sends specific drive-control commands, determines the drive's status, and passes the same data, but in a new format—a format appropriate for the disk drive's read/write channels.

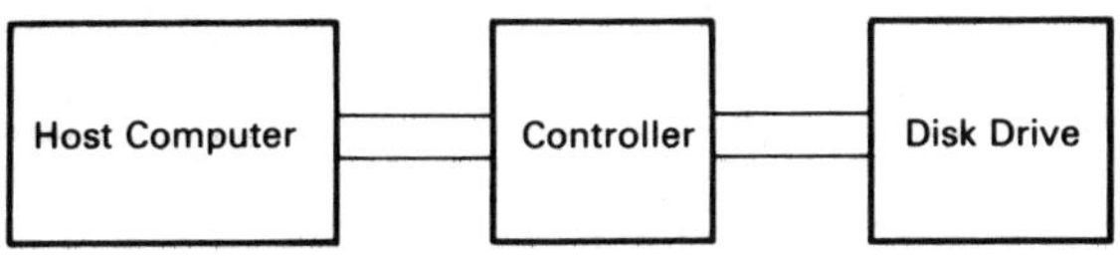

FIGURE 6–1
The disk controller comes between the disk and the host computer.

Not every controller has the same functionality. You wouldn't want them to, for not every system demands the same capability from the controller. Some offer the disk formatting as an integral part of their operation, some don't. Some controllers will include the data separator, others won't. Some have specialized host interfaces that suit specific computers. You might choose a controller such as Ackerman Digital Systems' Octafloppy that gives an S-100 bus computer floppy disk storage, for example. Other controllers offer generalized interfaces that adapt to various generic or intelligent computer bus structures. A controller might connect certain device interfaces to an IEEE-488 bus, or to a SASI/SCSI (Shugart Associates System Interface/ Small Computer System Interface) host interface. (More on these interfaces in Chapter 8.) If you use a controller with a generalized interface, typically you'll also require a circuit termed a *host adapter.* This host adapter translates the control lines and protocol of the generalized interface into terms that a particular computer understands. It converts the generalized interface into a specific interface. Thus, one generalized interface will work with any computer that has a host adapter. This provides a great deal of the sought-for device independence, or freedom from one manufacturer's hardware.

A specialized interface can offer some advantages over the generalized interfaces, however. It can take advantage of strengths in the computer's architecture. The controller designer will know in advance what the computer's interrupt structure is like, for example, and how the system is likely to service disk access commands. This information, used properly, can result in a system that requires less software to implement the disk subsystem.

Knowing the particulars of a computer's architecture, especially in more sophisticated systems, can even mean higher performance. In some systems, for example, the disk might have direct access to system memory. This *direct memory access* (DMA) allows the controller to pass data to the host computer's memory at high speed while the host does something else. When the data has been stored, the controller interrupts the system to let it know that the data

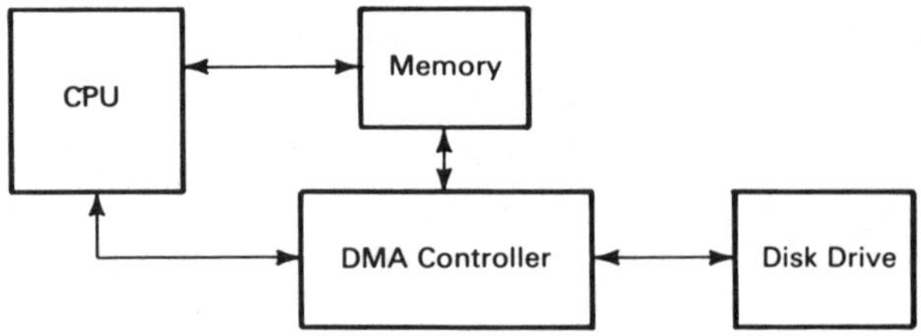

FIGURE 6–2
In a DMA system the controller has direct access to system memory.

is now available. And you can design a system to give several devices in one system the ability of making DMA transfers. The block diagram shown in Figure 6–2 is the general system configuration of a computer that uses DMA, but there are several techniques of implementing DMA.

You'll have to decide early in the design cycle whether you want each device controller to have its own DMA controller (this is the circuitry that gives the system its DMA capability) or if several device controllers will share one DMA controller. A number of system considerations (outside the scope of this book) will determine which is best. From the system integrator's point of view, however, separate DMA controllers allow each to operate independently.

The decision to use DMA doesn't have to result in a controller card designed for DMA, however. For some systems you can buy a DMA controller that controls the disk controller. A case in point is Rockwell International's Direct Memory Access Controller module (DMAC) shown in Figure 6–3. The controller handles transfers between an RM 65-based computer's memory and a variety of memory and I/O peripherals. The board's two 500K bit/sec data channels allow it to handle a double-density floppy disk controller easily, either interleaving data transfers with CPU operations or holding the CPU still for brief periods of high-speed burst mode data transfers.

Courtesy of Rockwell International.

FIGURE 6–3
Rockwell International's DMAC card gives RM 65 systems DMA capability.

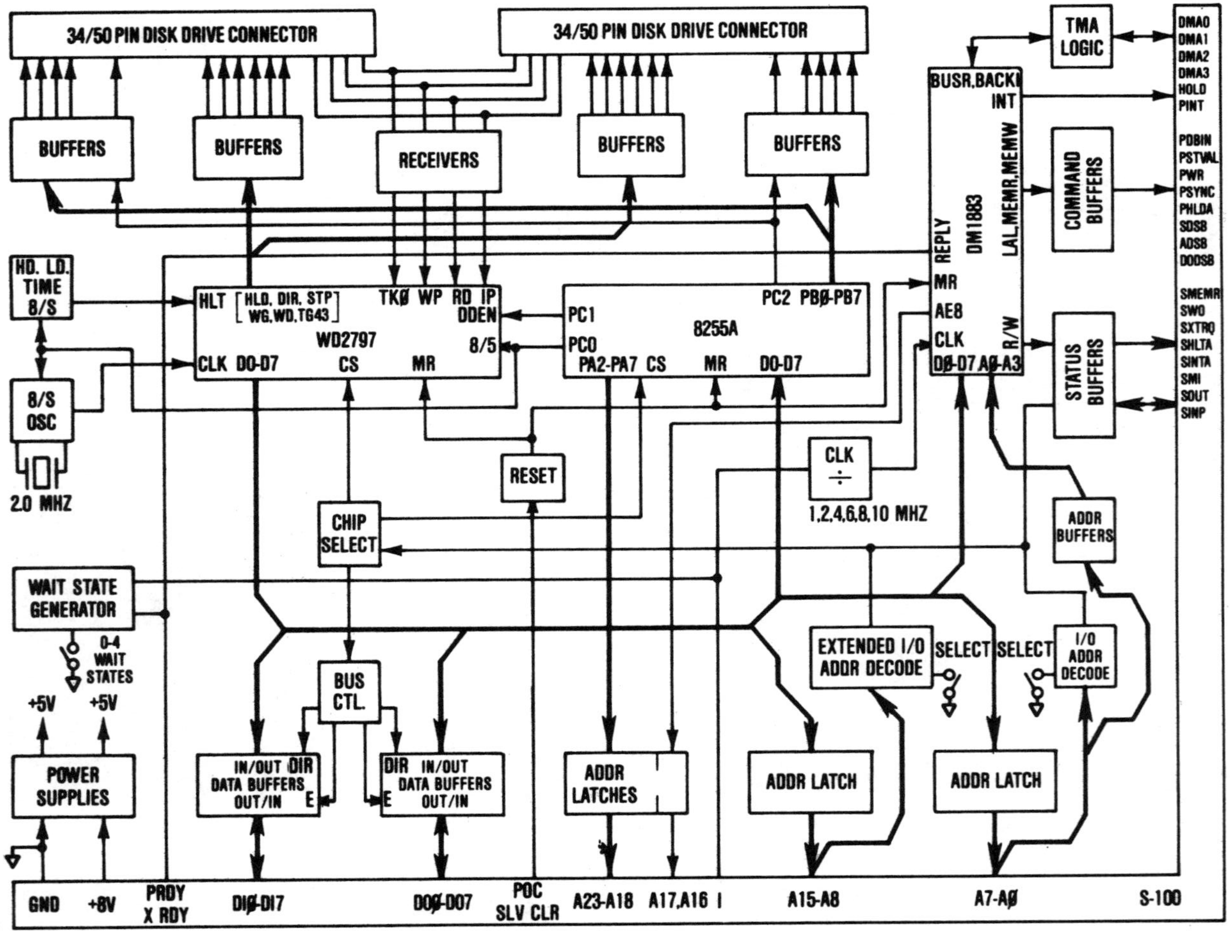

FIGURE 6–4
The Octafloppy controls up to eight floppy drives.

Courtesy of Ackerman Digital Systems.

Most controllers that use DMA will have the memory control circuitry onboard, however. Ackerman Digital Systems' Octafloppy controller, for example, uses an onboard DM1883 chip to map its eight floppies directly into the host computer's memory. The block diagram shown in Figure 6–4 shows the complete board.

Some controller manufacturers provide boards that give you multiple-drive control, DMA memory input and output, and still let you mix and match types of drives. This gives the system integrator the most flexibility in putting together a complete system while using a single controller.

The Disk 3 controller from CompuPro (Oakland, Calif.), for example, will handle up to four 5.25-in. Winchester disk drives. The controller plugs into an IEEE-696/S-100 bus computer and provides DMA with a switch-selectable interrupt priority. In this implementation the board will increase the performance of multiuser, multitasking computer systems immensely. The controller completely takes over the transfer of blocks of data to and from the disk, freeing the host computer for other system tasks. And, you can use the controller with a variety of manufacturer's drives, giving the system a variety of drive capacities and access times.

Any controller that is intelligent—that has its own microprocessor onboard—can manage block transfers. Simply allocate certain host memory addresses for the controller's use. The host computer then stores any data it wants put on the disk in the controller's address space and then tells the controller to write to the disk. Because the memory space would always be in the same location, the controller would never actually handle the data. It would simply read it from memory to the disk. In a read operation, it would reverse the process, passing data from the disk's read channel directly to the host's memory. This is basically what the Disk 3 does. Its operations, however, are tailored to the needs of an S-100 bus system.

Constructing a system that allows the CPU to just give the data over to a controller is thought of as making the transfers *transparent*. The system (the main computer) has no idea what happens to the data after it points it out to the controller. From then on the operation is invisible—transparent. The CPU can worry about some other system task.

Besides offering DMA, specialized interfaces help you enhance system performance in other ways. You can find interfaces that will let you replace several floppy disks with a single Winchester drive, for example. The system still sees the floppies, but physically these floppies are just space allocated on the Winchester drive. You get an increase in performance and reliability without having to change either the software or the operator's ways of doing business.

THE CONTROLLER FUNCTION

Regardless of the actual interface the system uses, the controller's job is to work in harmony with other system components, coordinating the activities of the disk with other system functions. In fact, a single controller will quite often control not just one disk, but several disks or various types (e.g., both Winchesters and floppies) and possibly a reel-to-reel or cartridge tape drive that will provide archival backup as well.

The controller accomplishes this feat by viewing each additional device as an addressable unit. The assumption is that only one device will be active at a time. To handle multiple devices, however, a controller will often need to store the data it receives from one device for some time before passing it on to the host computer or another peripheral. This means that either the controller must have some memory of its own (and all of the hardware that goes with that), or it must have access to some of the computer's memory to use for its own purposes. In other words the controller might make a DMA transfer of data to the memory space allocated to it and then not tell the host computer that the data is there.

Temporary Storage

Memory used in this fashion (as temporary storage) is referred to as *buffer space* or *buffer memory*. Most controllers will have some buffer space available, even if it's just used for holding the data while the controller does a CRC (cyclic redundancy check) on it. The CRC is a time-honored method of ensuring data integrity. The serial bit stream is divided by some predefined polynomial. The correct answer to this division exercise is stored along with the data. The processor does its own division on the data it receives and then compares its answer with the one it received. If they match, the processor assumes that it read the data properly.

Obviously, the more data manipulation (such as error detection and correction) that a controller does, the more buffer space it will need. And, if the controller is going to perform backup or data transfers at high speeds, it will need an interim place to store the data as it passes it from one device to the next. This problem springs up because the various system devices might not have exactly the same data transfer rates. The buffer space lets the system input and output to devices at their own pace—reducing the chance of errors.

The advantage of using memory in the host computer for this buffer space, rather than putting memory devices on the controller board itself, is that the amount of memory allocated to the task can change to accommodate the task at hand—it's flexible. Memory that is committed to the controller is useless (from a system standpoint) when you aren't using it for data transfers.

Although the practicality of this flexible buffer space depends on the rest of your system design (how much memory is available, etc.), the controller can keep the host advised on exactly how much space it needs and make unused space available to the rest of the system. You might even want to have one large buffer area divided up among several DMA controllers, with each reserving and using space and returning unused space to a common memory pool. The advantage to memory dedicated to a single peripheral or controller, on the other hand, is that it requires less management—the data will *always* pass through the same memory; thus, the data path can be hardwired—increasing access speed and minimizing the amount of system software required.

Thus, you can envision a controller as providing nearly every possible combination of disk control functions, from

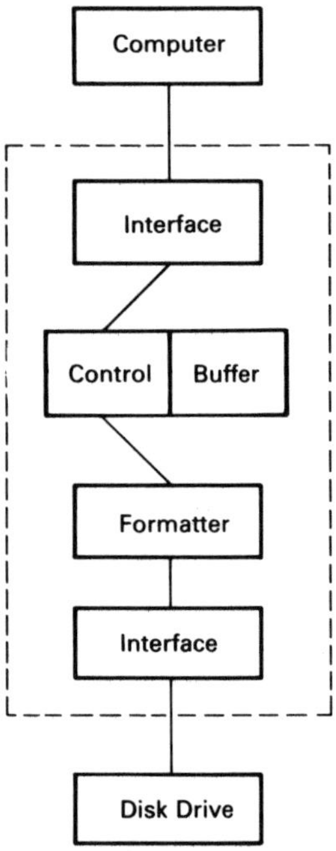

FIGURE 6–5
The controller performs a variety of functions.

a minimal "bare bones" controller that does the least amount of work possible to an intelligent controller that handles not only controller but formatting and interfacing (both to the computer and to the disk drive) functions with buffering. Interposed between the computer and the disk drive (or the formatter, if this is a separate unit), the controller's activities fall into the basic functions shown in the block diagram in Figure 6–5. Any of the modules within the dotted lines can be (and are) incorporated into a controller. And, for sophisticated controller applications, these individual functions can get extremely complex.

For any particular computer system you design, you will want to determine which of these functions should belong to the controller and which should properly belong to the host computer. Remember that *the rule of thumb* decrees that the more work the host computer does, the simpler the controller can be. The work must be done somewhere, however. This leads to two system-related drawbacks, however. If the host computer has to do too much of the disk control work, then it can't do other things. Disk access operations will bog down the computer. This is especially unhealthy if the computer has several simultaneous users. Furthermore, if you design too much of the controller's function into the host's software, it makes it much more difficult to change to another disk type when you want to upgrade the system's disk capacity or performance.

In order to define our minimum, or bare bones, controller, we must first break all of the disk I/O tasks into three basic categories. What is it that a disk must do? Then we can see the level of sophistication possible in each category. Regardless of its sophistication, the controller must provide the following:

- **Positioning control**—Control over the mechanics, especially the physical and electrical position of the heads
- **Read control**—Getting data from the disk into the computer's main memory
- **Write control**—Taking data from the computer's main memory and storing it on disk

Obviously these aren't job categories that can stand alone. This list just gives you the low-level command transfers and ignores the high-speed data interface, which will transfer data to and from the disk at a much faster rate than commands must be sent.

A single disk I/O operation easily uses control operations which fall within two separate control categories—positioning and, then, either read or write. To understand this sequence, let's look at the anatomy of a disk access command.

To read data from the disk, the computer might load one of the controller's registers with the desired track number, another with the desired sector number, and then issue a READ command. (You'll see the software explained in more detail in the next chapter. For now, we want to stick pretty much to the hardware side of things.) The controller must first seek the right location on the disk's surface, *positioning* the head over the proper track (or cylinder, in a multiplatter drive). This is a SEEK command. It seeks the appropriate track. Then the controller reads sector IDs, waiting until the proper sector comes along. Then it can *read* the data from the sector into the proper memory location. Notice that this simple operation managed to take us through two of our categories. A WRITE command reverses the process.

Now let's examine how a simple controller could perform each of these tasks in a real system. What, exactly, does the controller have to do?

A CONCRETE EXAMPLE

The disk, the formatter, and the controller comprise a complete disk subsystem that will typically sit right on the computer's data and control buses as shown in Figure 6–6. To the host the disk subsystem looks for all the world like just another place from which the computer can send or retrive data. The computer doesn't care if that hardware is a disk, a keyboard, a printer, or any other peripheral device. None of that matters because the controller will smooth out any differences in the way each peripheral operates.

For the purposes of illustration we are going to assume that the world is populated exclusively with 8-bit comput-

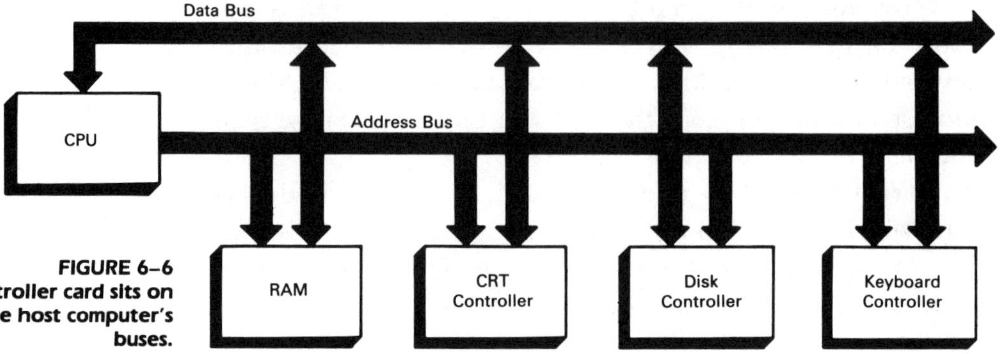

FIGURE 6–6
The controller card sits on the host computer's buses.

ers. There really isn't much more to working with 16-bit machines, but for the purposes of illustration, it is simpler to stay with a single design.

First, let's examine the components we will use to give our basic computer some disk storage. Almost every computer has a floppy disk, and it is an excellent device to use for illustration.

What do we need? First, we need the floppy disk itself. Since we want this to be a simple system for illustration purposes, let's choose a low-cost single-sided, single-density drive, such as the Siemens FDD 100-8. This drive is a standard 48-tpi 8-in. floppy that you can format in either single or double density. Using double-density encoding (MFM), it provides 6.4M bits (800K bytes) of storage and has a data transfer rate of 500K bits/sec.

The drive is simple enough that a low-level interface with just the control lines shown in Figure 6–7 will do everything we need. When the controller is given a disk access command, it tests the floppy's three static-level status signals to see if the drive can accept the command. These status levels indicate that a disk is loaded in the drive, and the drive is rotating at its operating speed (READY); WRITE PROTECT will signal that you can't write on the diskette that is mounted. (The term *mounted* means that the diskette is loaded in the drive. This comes from the days when computers all used reel-to-reel tapes which had to be mounted on a hub.)

If the logic of these three status levels indicates that all is in readiness, then the controller can issue a SELECT command (to enable all of the drive's input and output gates) and a HDLD (head load) command to put the heads into contact with the disk surface. Remember that this head load operation is unique to floppy disks. When you deselect a drive, the heads automatically unload (retract) to minimize head and disk wear.

With all of the gates enabled and the heads properly loaded, the controller can STEP the heads to the appropriate

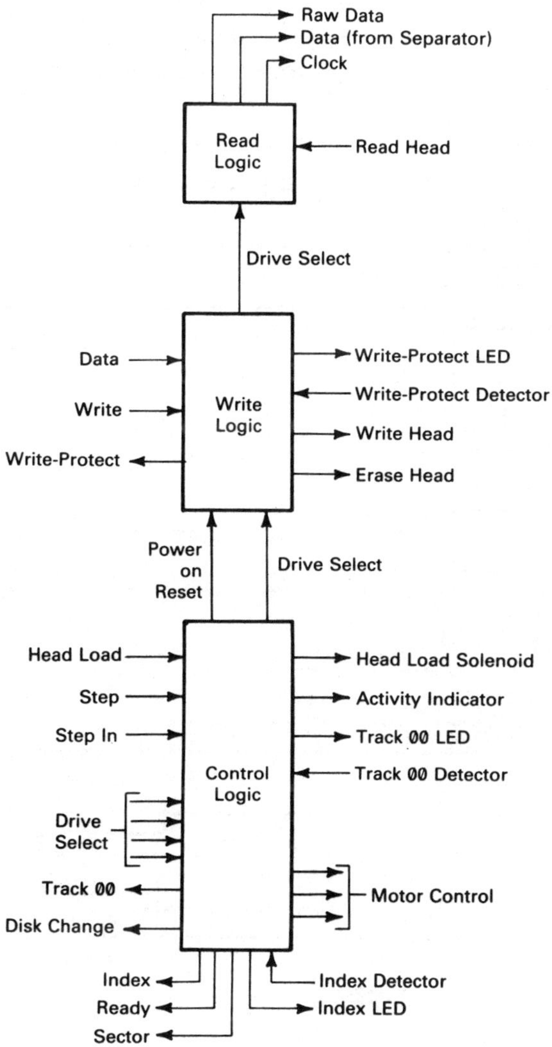

FIGURE 6–7
A low-level floppy interface.

track. One STEP pulse moves the heads one track—the direction (in or out) depending on the logic level of the STEP IN line. The diagram shown in Figure 6–8 gives the timing relationships of these signals.

Thus, the control functions are nothing more than loading the heads, selecting the drive, and stepping the heads to the appropriate track.

Getting the Data

Once the controller has put the heads into position and satisfied itself (by reading the sector ID information) that the data coming under the heads next is the data it was to read, the disk system has to get the data to the host computer. It's a basic two-step process: condition the data and transfer it.

The drive's MFM-encoding scheme necessitates a data separator to remove the clock pulses. If you use the drive in

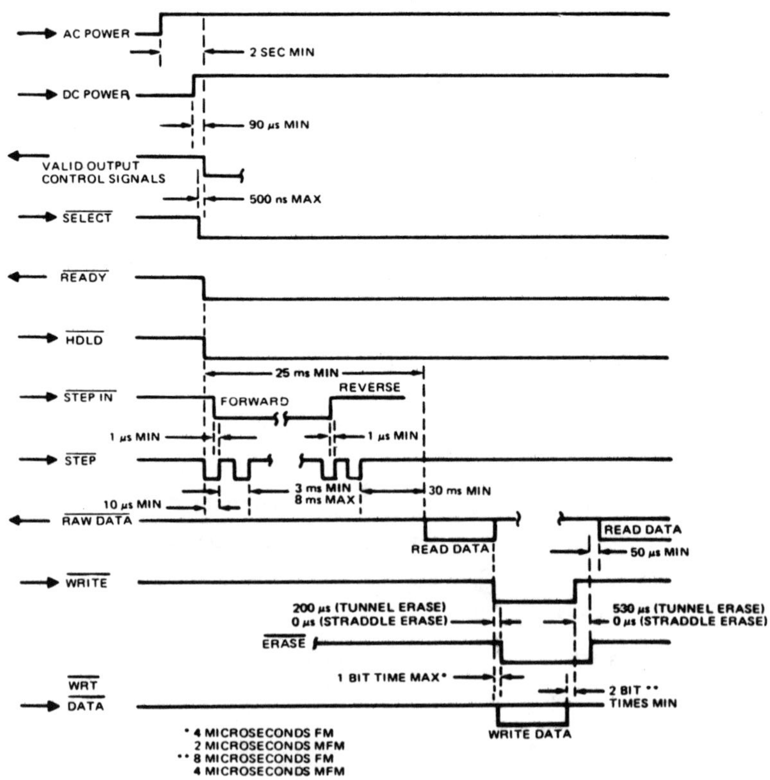

FIGURE 6–8
The timing of the floppy drive's control lines.

its single-density mode (FM), you can mount an optional data separator in the drive itself.

The read/write channel contains much of the circuitry it will need already. An LSI (large-scale integration) circuit provides such functions as a low write current control, a write current control, a high-gain read amplifier, a differentiating circuit that prepares the signals for the crossover detector, and a time-domain filter which disregards false zero crossings in the raw data. This circuitry converts what is basically an analog signal into a digital logic signal that the computer will understand.

To ensure the integrity of the data, you'll want the controller to add a bit of read/write logic (such as write-compensation logic) and preamplifiers. The block diagram for the complete read/write channel hardware is shown in Figure 6–9.

This is all of the hardware you need to control (and use) a simple floppy drive. It is the simplest possible controller. But, being practical, most systems require more features than this bare bones controller provides.

Adding a Second Drive

Unfortunately, for most applications you can't get away with just one drive—especially if it's a floppy drive. How would you make duplicate copies of disks so that you can protect your data or pass copies along to colleagues? You could write data into the host's main memory and then

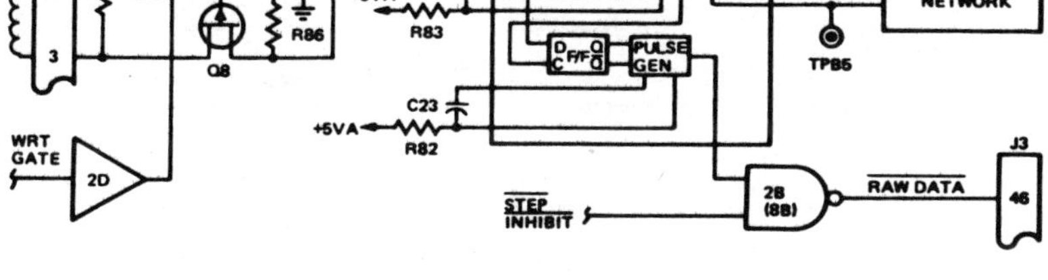

FIGURE 6–9
This is all of the read/write hardware you'll need.

change diskettes and write it back out. But to copy 800K bytes of data this way would take quite a bit of diskette swapping. You can do it that way, but it ties up the computer (you can't use the computer for anything else) and it is inconvenient.

A better solution is to add a second disk drive. This requires modifying the controller, but the job isn't as much trouble as you might think. We've already mentioned that some controllers can handle more than one drive, now we will see exactly how that works in practice. It really isn't complicated.

Take a look at the complete block diagram for the system we just designed (Figure 6–10). How much of this will we have to duplicate for the second drive? How much of this can do double duty? Fortunately, if the second drive is the same type as the first, much of the work is already done.

Assuming that the computer will only access one drive at a time (a safe assumption for most systems), two drives can easily share the same data paths (including the data separator) and the same control logic. The biggest problem facing our circuit is finding a way to tell which drive we want to talk to. The FDD 100-8 has an optional binary select logic that will allow you to multiplex, not just two, but up to eight drives. The SELECT 0 line enables the decoder logic; the lines labeled SELECT 1, 2, and 3 decode a binary address of 0 through 7. All the controller has to do, therefore, is give the binary select logic the number of the drive it wants to control. That drive remains selected until a new drive is selected.

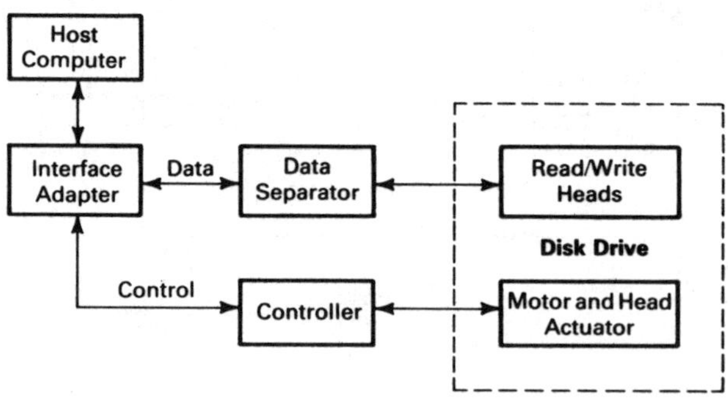

FIGURE 6–10
The compleat controller.

But what does it mean to select a drive? A deselected drive won't accept commands from the controller or give it status information. The logic levels would be present in all of the drives, but only the selected drive would respond. The binary number is the drive's address. Because the address remains consistent, this allows the user to access, not just disk storage, but a particular disk.

Upgrading the System

Not every new drive you add to a system will be from the same manufacturer, however. Even if you are adding a second floppy drive, you might choose one that uses a different encoding scheme or format. And, if you are serious about improving the performance of a system, sooner or later you'll consider putting a rigid disk on it. After all, the rigid disk will add both capacity and faster access times. These changes will have important repercussions in the controller design.

Consider the task of connecting a Winchester disk to a host computer. In this design example we will use the Vertex V100 series drive. Fully formatted (32 sectors of 256 bytes each), the Model V130 drive furnishes 24.3M bytes of formatted storage capacity. The drive has two platters and positions its heads with a rotary voice coil. One disk surface contains the servo data.

The controller will need some new control lines. The drive has four connectors: one handles control logic (J1); one provides data connections (J2); one is for power (J3); the last supplies frame ground (J4).

Data transfers take place at 5M bits/sec, and the data is encoded in an MFM scheme. Because the data isn't totally self-clocking, you'll still need a data separator to remove the clock pulses that do occur. It then seems that some of the old circuitry might be useful. But this data path has to operate at 10 times the speed that the floppy disk's path ran. In some cases the circuit you designed for the floppy drives will manage 5M bits/sec, but typically you'll need a new circuit that is designed for the higher speeds.

In most cases the best approach for taking care of both the need for extra control lines and accommodating the higher data transfer rate is to provide a device-independent interface. There are two such interfaces that might handle the Vertex drive: the ANSI standard proposed by the X3T9.3 committee and the enhanced small disk interface (ESDI). Using such an interface would mean that you gain the ability of mixing and matching a variety of Winchesters. We will discuss these interfaces more fully in Chapter 8.

Backing Up with Tape

The problem with the system we've got now is that it is going to take some time to backup (copy) all the data on the Winchester onto floppy disks. And the higher the Winchester's capacity, the worse the problem will be. Storing 35M bytes on double-density FDD 100-8 diskettes will take 44 diskettes. Current technology gives you two reasonable solutions. You can choose a Winchester drive that has a removable cartridge, such as DMA Systems' 5/5 (we discussed this drive in Chapter 2). This drive has a 5.25-in. disk in a removable cartridge and another it uses as a fixed disk. Each disk stores 5M bytes of data, so backing up the fixed disk is a simple matter of copying from the fixed disk to the removable cartridge. Because the disk has a 5M bit/sec data transfer rate, you can back up the entire fixed-storage area in 8 sec.

Not everyone is thrilled with the idea of removable Winchester media. It is relatively expensive to buy cartridges. Magnetic tape is a time-honored alternative. Reliable and inexpensive, magnetic tape is likely the most widely used backup media. The most efficient method of backing up with tape is to run the tape in its streaming mode—the tape runs constantly during the backup operation, making an exact copy of the disk on tape. It even leaves out the interrecord gaps that tape drives normally use to mark the beginning and end of records. It forfeits its own formatting in order to be able to store data quickly and reliably.

Regardless of how you choose to back up data, keep the complete system specification clearly in mind. And don't scrimp on the controller—it might make the difference between a system that is truly cost-effective and one that isn't.

7 The Software

You can have the best system hardware in the world and the best peripherals, but you don't have a computer system until you complete the system design with software. The software, it is said, at least by the system programmers I know, makes the hardware go. It's a statement that is hard to disprove.

In this chapter we deal with the system software, as opposed to application software. While application software will cause the system to carry out a particular task, it is the system software that specifically directs the hardware, instructing it in what to do. An accounts receivable program, for example, is an application package. An operating system is system software. An easy test to help determine which category of software you are dealing with is to ask, "Will the system do anything at all without this software?" If the answer is no, you are probably dealing with system software.

You don't really need to be a programmer to integrate a disk into your system; you can usually buy the software you need. But you will need to understand the software tasks involved in disk input and output in order to be able to intelligently specify and use the software you buy. Unfortunately, it isn't particularly easy to tell if you've got the right system software. There are no quick tests, no suitable benchmarks. Even determining the amount of software that it will take to control the disk drive you've added to your system varies. It depends on the sophistication of the disk subsystem. Some software works better for certain system configurations than others.

Short of becoming a programmer (a fate to be wished on no one, especially an engineer), your needs as a system integrator are best served by coming to terms with what the software does and only a little touch of how it does it.

Thus, we will avoid computer listings and keep things in terms of flowcharts and other machine-independent visual devices.

The easiest computer system to understand, and therefore the best illustration, is one that uses a popular (and somewhat generalized) operating system. CP/M® (which stands for control program/microcomputer) is a good example of this type of operating system.* It works with only a single user, and runs each program task (job) in order—one job at a time. In the jargon it is a single-tasking operating system.

This restriction is important for our analysis because the operating system always retains control over the flow of commands and data within the system. An operating system that was managing multiple tasks simultaneously would be too complex. In some systems the operating system will support several things going on concurrently (with a single processor they only *appear* to occur simultaneously). That's a bit much to deal with the first time through. Besides, the multitasking aspect doesn't really change the job that the software does, nor even how it does it. It only changes the order in which a few things happen.

TYING IT ALL TOGETHER

The operating system's function is that of tying all of the system's hardware components together and ensuring that it all runs in an orderly fashion. To help it do this, it has some generalized tools for dealing with peripherals. In Digital Research's CP/M, for example, you'll find these tools in

*CP/M® is a registered trademark of Digital Research Corporation, Pacific Grove, California.

the parts of the operating system known as the basic input-output system (BIOS) and the basic disk-operating system (BDOS). Together, these two components form the FDOS (floppy disk operating system). The FDOS is hardware dependent. That means that it needs an explicit description of the hardware that it uses. The description is in the form of values, or *parameters,* which give the software the information that it needs. Giving the operating system these descriptive values is known as *system configuration.*

To bring the idea into sharp focus, let's consider one specific example of a disk parameter that the operating system would obviously need to know about. If you are using direct memory access (DMA)—passing data straight into memory from the disk without the processor handling the data—the processor will need to know which memory locations the controller is storing the data in. Without this address information the processor would never find the data.

Within the CP/M operating system, Function 26 sets the DMA address. CP/M normally sets this address to 0080 (hex) over the boot address. But you can change this default address (the value a parameter has, unless you change it, is referred to as a *default value*) to another memory location. This function is a standard mechanism for giving the processor the address.

Other standard operating system functions you'll find in operating systems include the following:

- Disk system reset
- Drive selection
- File creation
- Directory search
- Interrogate available disks

In all, the version of CP/M that suits 8-bit microcomputers has 38 of these I/O functions. Other operating systems will feature more or less, depending on their sophistication and the way that they handle I/O. And for each function there will be some parameters, or characteristics, that you will have to supply when you configure the system. It looks like the operating system is going to require a lot of information, and it does. But where does it store this data? Most operating systems have some sort of disk parameter tables which store, among other things, the address of disk parameter blocks (DPB). These blocks contain detailed information about your disk drive, such as the number of sectors per track, the total capacity of the disk, the number of directory entries that you can store on the drive (the maximum number of files that you can put on the disk), and the size of the directory check vector. When you configure your system, you are actually putting the appropriate information in the disk parameter block. Later you'll see how storing that information helps the operating system do its job.

The information that the operating system requires is quite detailed. You are going to have to get to know your disk drive well in order to tell the operating system how to talk to it. Sometimes all of the information that you need won't even be in the manual supplied with the drive. You might have to contact the manufacturer's customer support group to get the information.

Yet, without this information, which is stored in tables, it wouldn't be possible for one operating system to control a variety of disks. You'd need unique software for every combination of system peripherals. Any problems that the configuration process might give you are certainly more than compensated for by the flexibility it gives you.

DRIVING THE DISK

Let's take a hard look at the way the operating system treats data input and output. When it has data that it wants to send to the disk, or when an application program requests data from the disk, it makes a disk I/O request. The operating system calls a software module (or routine) that will actually handle the I/O device. This procedure, shown in Figure 7–1, is termed *servicing* the I/O request.

These operating system modules, known as *device drivers,* are, in one sense, specialists. One driver is designed to

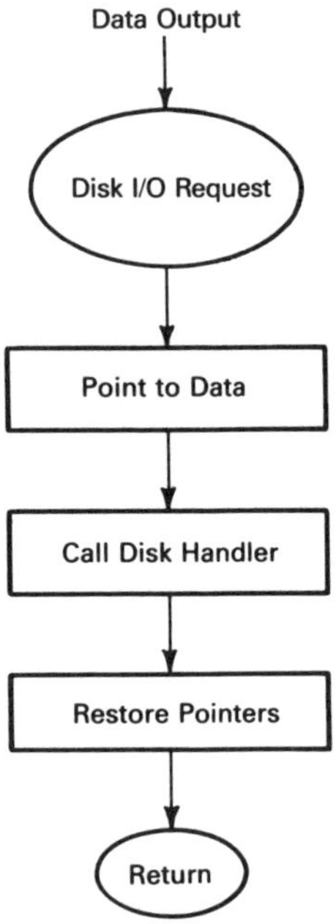

FIGURE 7–1
Input and output are handled with special software.

handle disk drives, one handles the keyboard, another handles console devices, and so on. There is a device driver for each of the operating system's logical devices. When you assign a logical device name to a physical (actual) device, the operating system will then know to call that device driver when it wants to use the physical device assigned to it.

The device driver handles data passing to and from the disk and converts system requests into disk commands. Typically, this means that the driver will contain the explicit conversion of system disk commands into device-dependent disk commands. The driver essentially acts as an interpreter that resides between the operating system and the disk hardware (the controller), as shown in Figure 7–2.

Another way to look at the device driver routine is as a very short application program. It performs its specific task (either writing or reading data), returns control to the main program, and then goes away until it is needed again. Each time that the program uses the disk, it calls the routine again.

Each time the routine is called, it gets the device-dependent particulars of its instructions—the disk's operating parameters—directly from the disk parameter block and performs the required operations.

In the sense that the software has no allegiance to any particular hardware, the device driver is an extremely generalized program. It can handle a myriad of disk types because its operations are deliberately generalized to handle different disk drive characteristics. This is important because it lets you buy the operating system you want, and the drive

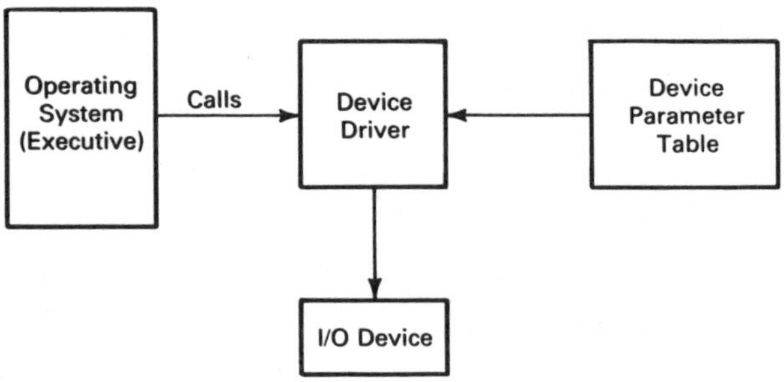

FIGURE 7–2
The device driver contains the hardware-specific I/O routines.

you want, and worry about making the two work together later on.

The Sum of Its Parts

Although its basic function is fairly straightforward, the disk driver is a sophisticated program. Our exposure to it thus far has been, necessarily, oversimplified. The driver looks, at this point, like a program which can

- Send data to the disk
- Retrieve data from the disk

But it does more than just this. Even a simple driver must also be able to

- Initialize the disk
- Format the disk

Effectively carrying out these two tasks is not trivial. Not if it is to implement them properly.

A typical device driver actually consists of not one, but several, interwoven routines. The effectiveness of the software in dealing with the disk depends, to some extent at least, on how many commands the controller can execute directly and how many the driver must break up into smaller pieces. By a *typical* controller, we choose to mean one that handles a rigid disk. One that includes just a few basic commands but operates over a parallel interface. (The use of a parallel interface eliminates most of our worry over the data transfer rate.)

Using the controller's command repertoire intelligently can save you a great deal of coding. If the controller understands the command FORMAT, for example, then the actual amount of code required for formatting the disk is much simpler than it would be otherwise. But now the driver must be written such that it knows that this command exists. Take a look at the basic flowchart for the format routine shown in Figure 7–3.

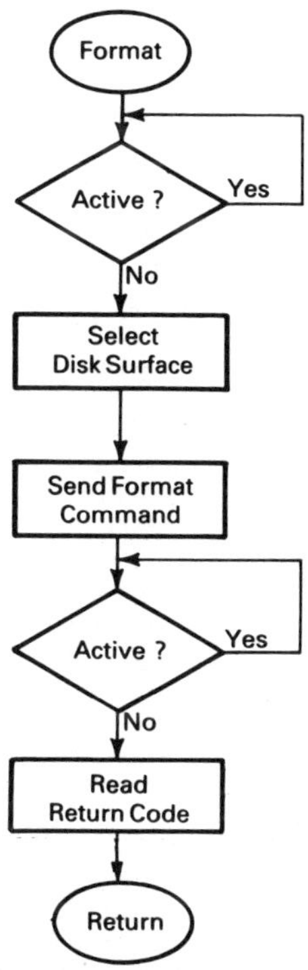

FIGURE 7–3
Formatting the disk is simple if the controller has a FORMAT command.

This simple flowchart works for a code that assumes there exists a format command that the controller understands. All the device driver must do, therefore, is select the desired disk surface (A or B) and send the format command (along with the drive number) to it. Naturally, if there are more than two surfaces available, the software will need to know this too.

After the disk is formatted, the routine reselects the same disk surface, sets it for input, and reads a return code from the controller. This return code is a condition code—it contains any errors that the controller encountered while formatting the disk. If a sector is bad, or the formatter couldn't use a track and had to pick an alternate track to take its place, for example, the return code would have to indicate that the track was bad. The format routine would then take care of selecting the alternate track and renumbering the tracks.

Without this formatting command the routine would have to step the disk drive through the complete formatting process, as follows:

- Move the heads to track 0
- Reset all error conditions
- Write the track with known data
- Read and verify the data
- Repeat the entire process for the next track

and so on, until the entire surface has been erased and tested.

The trade-off here is the same that you'll find in any other aspect of the system design—you can do the task in the host computer, or you can distribute the system's intelligence into its peripherals.

Obviously, the more commands you want to put into the peripheral, the simpler the job of device I/O is for the host computer. It can pass the data to the controller and say, "Here, you do it." A rich command set for the host computer is like a good, high-level language for a programmer. It lets him accomplish a lot with few instructions. The command set essentially moves the device driver, or parts of it, out into the peripheral.

Two other important commands in the device driver's bag of tricks take care of the READ and WRITE operations. Even though both of these are also in the controller's command set, there is a certain amount of *housekeeping* that the driver has to do to get the proper data to the proper place. These commands will operate on a complete sector of disk data at a time—that is why the disk parameter block must contain the sector size. Whether the disk uses sectors that contain 128 bytes or 512 bytes, the routine must allocate enough memory space to write a complete sector.

Issuing the WRITE command to the controller causes it to write a complete sector of data to the disk. But where does this data come from? It must first be stored in the disk buffer. The host computer must write the data into a buffer somewhere and then pass that information to the device driver. (As we discussed in Chapter 6, this buffer memory can be either in the host system or on the controller.) Before it can do this, of course, it needs to know how big a sector is.

After creating and filling the buffer, the device driver issues a WRITE command, passing the buffer pointer (the byte that points to the buffer memory) and the drive, track, and sector numbers (the destination location) to the controller. This is all the information the controller needs to store the data safely on the disk.

Here's how the controller handles the data. When it sees a WRITE command from the host computer, the controller ensures that the drive, track, and sector numbers are valid. This means that it compares them against the list of all possible values for drive and sector. It won't test to see if the values are right, however. The controller has no way of knowing what the right sector is.

If the values are valid, the controller enables the drive—that is, it seeks the correct track and reads sector ID until it finds the right sector—and writes the data to it. Then it reads the data to ensure the data's integrity. Is it what you sent to the disk?

The results of this integrity check are formed into a return code that tells the host system how the write operation went. The host computer can then decide whether to rewrite the sector or move on to other things. The flowchart shown in Figure 7–4 illustrates the complete interaction of the WRITE command.

But there are some interesting specifics in the WRITE routine. Notice the GETBUF routine shown in Figure 7–5. This routine is the one that actually takes data from the disk buffer and reads it to the disk. The routine loads one of the processor's registers with a byte that contains the data buffer's location and then strobes the data from the buffer to the data bus. It moves one byte at a time, counting the number of iterations. When the number of bytes sent to the disk equals the number of bytes in a sector (from the disk parameter block), the WRITE routine resumes control of the operation.

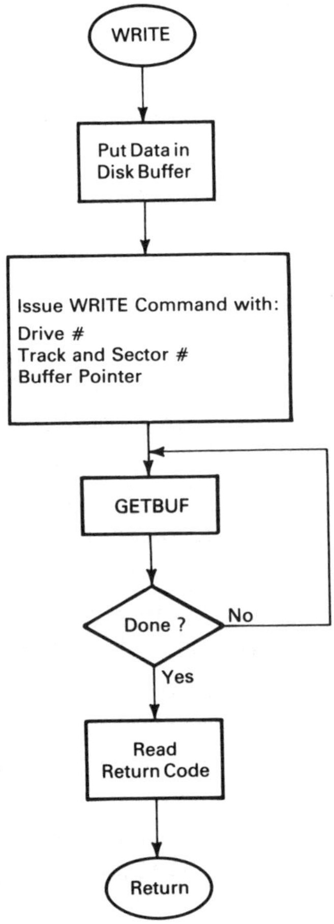

FIGURE 7–4
The WRITE command writes a complete sector, one byte at a time.

The READ command (Figure 7–6) logic is quite similar to that of the WRITE command. It reads a sector of data from the disk to the buffer, one byte at a time. By counting the number of bytes, the routine can calculate when it has read every sector. The return code is, of course, read before the data, in this case.

THE WELL-FOCUSED SYSTEM

Now you've seen all of the routines that make up a standard device driver for disk drives. And, if you are designing turnkey systems focused on a specific application, you've probably seen many opportunities for tightening up the code. You can certainly choose to optimize the routines for a particular hardware set.

Code optimization will certainly speed up the system's operation. Writing just the code that a particular controller/drive combination requires means that you can eliminate some steps and disregard leaving provisions for other capabilities. You could, for example, eliminate the disk parameter blocks. If you know well in advance that you'll only

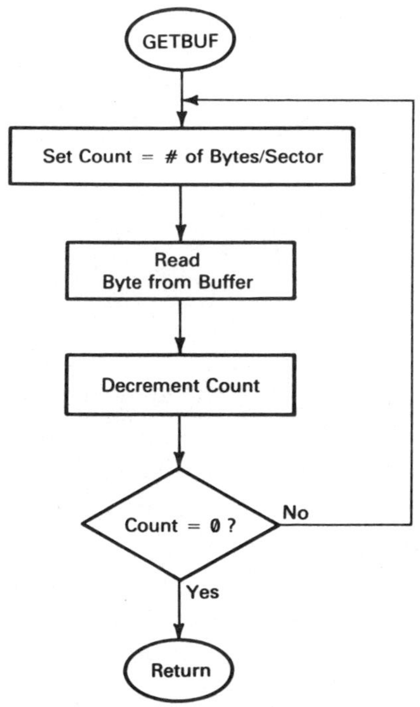

FIGURE 7–5
The GETBUF routine loops until it has read the entire sector.

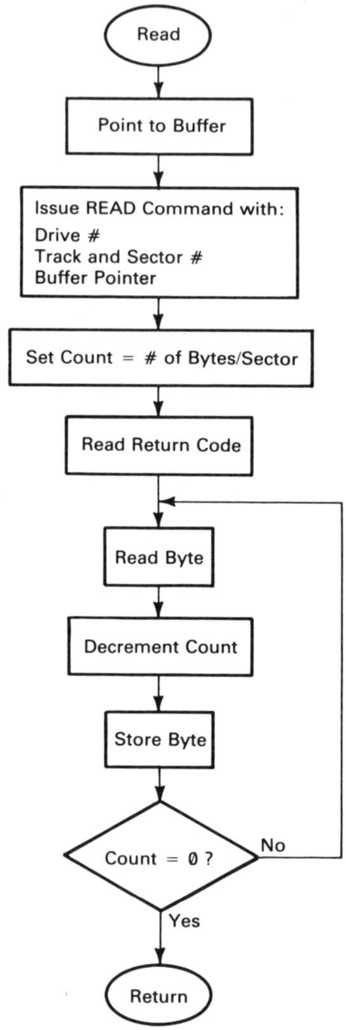

FIGURE 7–6
The READ command reverses the write operation.

run a certain disk drive with the system, you can save memory and execution speed by embedding the sector size in the device driver. Then, instead of having to look up the current number of bytes per sector, number of drives, or disk surfaces (or anything else that doesn't change too frequently), the routine can simply begin executing. This gives you many opportunities to get rid of unnecessary code. If you take this approach, you'll have what is commonly termed a *tightly coupled* system.

There's a danger here, of course. If you, or the end user, ever do decide to upgrade the system's disk capacity, you'll have to change the disk parameters everywhere they are used. With the more generic disk parameter block, you change the values in a single location. Which you should choose depends entirely on what the system constraints are. **Just remember the trade-off is speed and code size for flexibility.**

BUYING DRIVERS

In many cases you won't have to write your own drivers at all. Unless your requirements are rather exotic, why should you? Not only do operating systems, such as CP/M, come with device-independent drivers, you can often buy device-independent drivers for other operating systems. Software and disk controller vendors make drivers available for operating systems as diverse as Intel's iRMX™ (real-time operating system), Xenix, and various minicomputer operating systems. As before, the device independence comes from the fact that you will have to provide the operating system with information about the disk drive you choose. Look closely at the configuration capability of these drivers, however. Some have extremely clever configuration software that makes reconfiguring your system a breeze—such as the interactive configuration program from Dilog we saw in the Chapter 5—especially the drivers that come from some of the controller vendors. But such programs aren't system software as such. They are utilities—development tools that you'll use only when you change the system hardware. If you intend to purchase a variety of drive types, however, such a tool can make short work of an otherwise troublesome task.

Whether you write your own drivers, modify someone else's, or buy off-the-shelf software, the key word to remember is *harmony*. Insist that all of the system components—both hardware and software—be harmonious. The software is not a good place (if there is a good place) just to make do. If the components are harmonious, you'll not only have an easier time building your system but maintenance will be easier too.

CONNECTION AND PROTOCOL III

8 The Compleat System

The first two parts of this book have pretty well covered the disk as a system device, per se. Now it's time to round out our perspective. We must move further into the area of system integration—the art of making all of our evaluation and analysis pay off. How do we get the disk functioning as an integral part of the system? Here we must (once again) break the available choices down into two separate strategies and evaluate each one separately.

The first, and usually the easiest, technique is not to buy a disk at all. Instead of creating a disk subsystem for your host computer, you can buy prepackaged disk subsystems

FIGURE 8–1 A disk subsystem for Hewlett-Packard computers.

Courtesy of Bering Industries.

that will plug directly into some port on the computer. This subsystem approach isn't usually the most cost-effective way to build a system, but it has significant merits which you should keep in mind.

THE SUBSYSTEM APPROACH

The subsystem is a labor-saving product. Just as buying a single-board computer saves you the work of designing your computer at the component level, the disk subsystem saves you the work of designing the disk hardware. All that you have to worry about is selecting the proper unit and integrating it into the system—not frivolous concerns, to be sure.

The products that you have to choose from are, with few exceptions, extremely specialized. They are meant to work with a particular host computer in a certain way. The designers of the subsystems usually are extremely knowledgeable concerning the interaction of the disk with a narrow range of computers, but often out of their depth when asked to go much beyond that. Thus, products that work especially well with an Apple® computer, for example, might not work at all with an AIM® 65, even though both are 6502-based machines.*

Subsystems also give you a great deal of flexibility. You can pick from a range of storage devices and capacities, so you can opt for more or less the performance you want.

Take, for example, the disk subsystem from Bering Industries shown in Figure 8–1. Intended to compete with the computer manufacturer's offerings, this device gives Hewlett-Packard computers an economical Winchester disk drive

*Apple® is a registered trademark of Apple Computer, Inc., Sunnyvale, California. AIM® is a registered trademark of Data Processing Consulting, Inc., Boulder, Colorado.

and can also furnish a floppy disk for data backup and software distribution.

Although using Bering's Series 3000 subsystem does limit your choices of the disk drive your system will have, you can still select 5, 10, or 15M bytes of Winchester storage; the floppy drive can be a 3.5-, 5.25-, or an 8-in. drive. Furthermore, the subsystem is configured such that several (two or three) computers can share the disk subsystem. In fact, there are 20 basic configurations of the subsystem. That is a fair amount of versatility. But it costs. Unless the subsystem manufacturer is also a disk drive manufacturer (rare), you'll be paying a markup on the disk itself as well as paying for the packaging. The price may well be worth it, however, especially if you are working on a tight design schedule. The commercially available subsystem will represent a known quantity in such cases.

Other subsystems are available for providing disk storage for nearly every popular computer imaginable, including Apple, Heath/Zenith™, Commodore™, and TRS-80®. Or, you can select subsystems that work with a particular computer bus structure, such as Multibus®, S-100 bus machines, and so on.*

If you choose to pick a subsystem by computer type, start your search with the computer manufacturer. Even if you don't like what you see, you'll get an idea of what is possible and at what price. Apple Computer, for example, provides both one- and two-disk (floppy) subsystems called, appropriately, Unifile™ and Duofile™, that give an Apple III up to 1,742,848 bytes of online storage (Figure 8–2).†

When a computer is as popular as the Apple, you'd be foolish to stop here. Scan through any computer magazine and you'll see dozens of ads for Apple peripherals. Compare the prices and capabilities, and you might find exactly the subsystem you want at an affordable price.

---

*Heath/Zenith™ is a trademark of Heath Corporation. Commodore™ is a trademark of Commodore Business Machines, King of Prussia, Pennsylvania. TRS-80® is a registered trademark of Radio Shack, a division of the Tandy Corporation.

†Unifile™, Duofile™, and Apple III are trademarks of Apple Computer, Inc., Sunnyvale, California.

Courtesy of Apple Computer.

FIGURE 8–2
Apple users have a choice of one- or two-disk subsystems.

A WEALTH OF CHOICES

Selecting one subsystem might be the hardest part of using this design approach. Much of the design work that you are paying for is obscured by claims of high performance. And there is a great deal of variation in design quality. Some of these subsystems come in extremely sophisticated and clever packages, where a great deal of attention has been paid to ensuring that the result will be a reliable system component.

In the StacPac family from Data Systems Design, for example, even the cabling is routed to reduce the effects of radiated noise and to eliminate cable clutter (an amazingly frequent cause of system failures). Other subsystems might be equally well designed and executed or merely put the disk, controller, formatter, interface, and support components in a pretty package. For some designers the packaging alone is worth the price.

Depending on your particular design skills, your manufacturing capability, and the number of computer systems you'll be producing, you can choose to let others do a great deal of the work for you.

PLUG COMPATIBILITY

As your performance needs go up, the problems of mass storage become increasingly hard to solve. This is why system design must be pursued from the top (the overall performance specifications) down to the components. You must match the total system performance to the application, and you can't do this on a piecemeal basis. Consider the problem of the application which requires the computing power of a minicomputer.

In the world of minicomputers, selecting the proper mass storage gets extremely tricky. There is a large amount of commercial software available to minicomputer users, but only if the hardware configuration meets certain expectations. Minicomputer operating systems have been stable for some time now, and the disk drives are taken as a given. The manufacture of disk subsystems is, therefore, quite specialized, and you'll find vendors selling subsystems that conform to the software. These subsystems might contain a variety of Winchester disks from a number of manufacturers, but the system won't know it. Only the user's pocketbook will see the difference. The subsystem manufacturer's claim to fame is that the subsystem makes these drives look to the host computer like disk systems that the computer manufacturer also provides.

Why bother? Why not just buy the disks that are supposed to be used with the computer?

There are two basic arguments for plug-compatible disk subsystems: The minicomputer companies don't necessarily have the best prices for peripherals, and it's nice to have a second source for just about anything you intend to buy in volume. Plug-compatible peripherals, especially in the form of subsystems, satisfy both requirements. Because they look like the original equipment, you can use them to upgrade a system without paying the price (or waiting out the lead time) that the computer manufacturer imposes.

Any attempt at plug compatibility, if it's going to work at all, has to be 100 percent. The idea is to let the system integrator put these subsystems to work with almost no work other than simple installation—usually little more than plugging in a board. This is the world of plug-compatible systems, and it usually involves Digital Equipment Corporation or Data General minicomputer systems.

Some controller manufacturers intend to make it easy for you to piece together your own plug-compatible subsystems. Distributed Logic Corporation, for example, offers a controller that lets you build a disk subsystem for DEC's LSI-11 computers, giving the host a variety of disk capacities ranging from two 8M-byte drives to two 300M-byte drives. The DQ215 board plugs directly into the computer's backplane and makes your drives look like DEC's RK06/07 drives. The board works with three of DEC's most popular operating systems without requiring any software changes at all. The system software doesn't know the difference between drives that *are* RK06s and drives that only *appear* to be those drives.

Sigma Information Systems' SDC-RLV22 interfaces with Xebec's S1410 formatter to allow a 5.25-in. Winchester drive to emulate DEC's RL01/RL02 disk subsystem at far less money than you'd pay for an RL01 subsystem. The hardware is transparent to the DEC operating system—the existing device drivers work fine.

If you aren't directly replacing an existing system drive, you'll need to find device drivers for your subsystem. Most subsystem manufacturers can either supply or recommend appropriate software drivers that will take the worry out of system integration altogether. Assuming you have a reasonably standard system. Assuming you can afford the complete subsystem. Assuming . . . well, you get the idea.

Off-the-shelf software has to be generic. Prepackaged solutions are, by definition, prepackaged. They will give you less variety to choose from, hence less flexibility in your system design, and less chance to create a better than average system. But, they will be simple to use.

DO IT YOURSELF

If you want to get something out of the ordinary from your computer system's performance, or you have a nonstandard system (e.g., one with a proprietary bus structure), you don't have any choice in the matter. You'll have to build your own system hardware—come up with circuits that meet your exact needs, whether those needs are in terms of packaging or performance. You could repackage a subsystem, but it wouldn't make good economic sense. Always remember that good engineering is as much a matter of economics as physics. That is why the term *cost-effective* crops up more than once in almost every engineering text.

This doesn't mean that you'll be building everything from scratch—or even that you'll actually build anything from scratch. The days of kludge cards and hard-wired breadboards seem far behind the system integrator, unless you want to get into the business of providing some value-added interface circuitry, that is.

Given the adaptable nature of the available circuits, such as controllers, your job should simply be to bundle together the appropriate formatter-controller and software along with the disk. And, in the case of a proprietary bus, you might have to come up with some interface circuitry. You certainly won't find it on a standard controller card. However, there are ways to minimize the interface problem, too. We will get to that later on in this chapter.

SOME SYSTEM INTEGRATION RULES

Understanding how to pick the optimum components is an important key to getting the most out of your system.

1. Pick the proper disk for the application. This rule sounds obvious, but it might be the hardest one to actually apply. During the time when you are analyzing the system to determine exactly what its needs are, one question that will come up is how much storage space does the system need. How much is enough?

Following right behind this question comes, how fast must the disk access be. There are some general answers to these questions. For a single-user system a 5- or 10M-byte drive might be more than enough. For a multiuser system (several users sharing one disk drive), you'll probably need a disk that gives you more than 50M bytes.

An access time of 85 msec suits any operation that doesn't require a lot of disk accesses, but a shared disk (our beloved multiuser system again with its four to eight users) should have average access times of less than 35 msec, or the individual users will have to spend a fair amount of time waiting for their disk access to be processed. The system will visibly slow down when all of its users are getting information from the disk. These numbers aren't absolutes; but the experience of system designers who have put together a few of these indicates that they are a pretty good place to start from. An important corollary to Rule 1 is: *Buy only as much disk as you need!*

The faster a disk's response time is, as a rule, the more it will cost. You can count on that rule being around for some time. Performance always costs. The same goes for capacity. And, the faster the disk access time, the faster the response time of the controller and other associated components. A high-capacity disk requires an interface with a high data transfer rate.

Remember that getting the data from here to there in a timely manner is at least as important as storing it reliably. High performance doesn't end with a single component. It's a system consideration.

The rule also applies to the disk's physical size, but inversely. The same capacity in a smaller package tends to cost more. If you have space problems, by all means look at getting 5M bytes in a small package, such as the Cricket from CDC (Figure 8-3). But the same capacity in an ST506

Courtesy of Control Data Corp.

FIGURE 8–3
The Cricket puts 5M bytes of storage in a 3.5-in. package.

will cost substantially less because the larger drive won't have to push the technology. It won't require plated media, for example, as the Cricket does.

Once again, keep the overall system concept in mind. A low-cost system can't easily afford to push the state of the art in technology. A high-performance, compact system can't afford to do anything less. It's all a matter of what you are trying to achieve. If your low-cost system looks like everyone else's, it might make sense to offer increased disk capacity or a hard disk instead of a floppy. But will the market stand for the extra costs involved? Your market research, rather than engineering sense, will have to help you decide.

2. Keep an eye on the new products. As disk capacities increase, users are demanding more and more disk capacity. Capacity is addictive. Programs follow Parkinson's law: They expand to fill the space allotted to them. Because 10M bytes don't cost that much more than 5M bytes, 5M-byte drives might not be around much longer.

And, low-capacity Winchesters with a 14-in. diameter are virtually extinct. The larger disks consistently move upward in capacity to find new markets—places where their size can be put to use—as the 5.25-in. drives invade the market for storage up to 50M bytes.

The disk drive market remains dramatically in flux. The best industrial soothsayers can't tell you reliably what will be around next year. If you are going to do all of the system integration job, you'd better spend some time evaluating the latest products available. The newest drives might prove far superior to the previous models in terms of their price or performance or both.

3. Don't do more work than you have to. This rule sounds a bit tongue in cheek, but it isn't. This is one of the more popular system integration rules. It is another way of getting us into the one bugaboo that we've mentioned, but avoided until now—the interface. Of course, your own system design will tell you how much you can use off the shelf and how much you'll have to do yourself. But never reinvent the wheel. The other axiom is: Just because you didn't design the circuit doesn't mean it's no good. Look at other designers' work with an open mind.

THE INTERFACE

Unless you're intent on designing for yourself perfectly good circuits that you can buy, you've got two basic choices in selecting an interface. The first choice is to buy a controller that exactly suits your needs, including matching your Mark III computer to the ever-popular Mark II disk drive. This gives you a plug-it-in-and-go solution which is quite nice. There are innumerable controller vendors. If you have a popular computer and want to use popular disks, you are all set. But what do you do if the choices are few and unpleasant? Not everyone designs controllers the way you want them to. There are some ways to expand your choices.

THE SYSTEM INTERFACE

There's an old joke in computer circles about the computer that was designed to meet established standards. This is a joke only because, for the most part, standards in the computer business (especially concerning peripherals) are every bit as solid and reliable as submarines at submarine races. Take 5.25-in. Winchester drives, for example. What is the standard interface?

If you are talking about low-capacity drives, then the standard is the ST506 interface we saw earlier. What happens if you upgrade your system to a higher-capacity drive such as a 70M-byte drive? Now you must choose an interface for yourself. There are ESDI (enhanced small disk interface) and ANSI (American National Standards Institute) proposals, but no agreement on which one to use. And the ANSI standard is the one proposed for 8-in. Winchesters that no one used. Sheer chaos.

Why such confusion? The industry has moved quickly in bringing products to market. Too quickly for interface standards to be developed (the standardization process can take years). But all is not lost. Enter the system standard.

The system standard creates an artificial system that

then becomes the standard. One such standard is the SASI (Shugart Associates System Interface), now called the SCSI (Small Computer System Interface). The standard represents an intelligent interface which can then be interfaced to a number of disk interfaces. Rather than interfacing a peripheral to a computer port, as we did in the Chapter 6, this approach is to interface an intelligent controller to the computer and then allow the controller to handle a variety of peripherals.

The block diagram shown in Figure 8–4 illustrates the elements of an SASI/SCSI controller. Actually, this defines a local I/O bus for disk drives. As was the case in previous controllers, this controller converts processor disk access commands into specific disk controls. But now the controller sits directly on the processor's bus.

The specific circuitry that interfaces the controller to the host processor is termed the *host adapter*. This hardware is the only part of the controller you would have to design, since it will be specific to your system. Once you define the adapter, you can then choose to use any controller that conforms to SCSI specifications.

Using a system standard widens your choices immensely. A number of vendors offer SCSI controllers. For example, Xebec has components that conform to standards from both ANSI to SCSI. Other firms are evaluating connections from ESDI to SCSI. And nearly everyone connects ST506 drives to SCSI interfaces. ADES has an entire family of SCSI host adapters and peripherals to choose from. The situation is analogous to the generic drivers themselves. You get flexibility for the price of generalizing. Drives become logical, rather than physical, devices.

If you have layout problems, don't worry. You can buy chip sets, such as Adaptec's ACS-4000 chip set which gives you compatibility between the SCSI standard (ANSI X3T9.2) and Seagate ST506 drives. Or, if you want to design your own circuits, the standard is well defined.

Then, if you upgrade to a higher-capacity disk later on, you will only need to change to a controller that supports whatever disk interface the new disk requires. The host

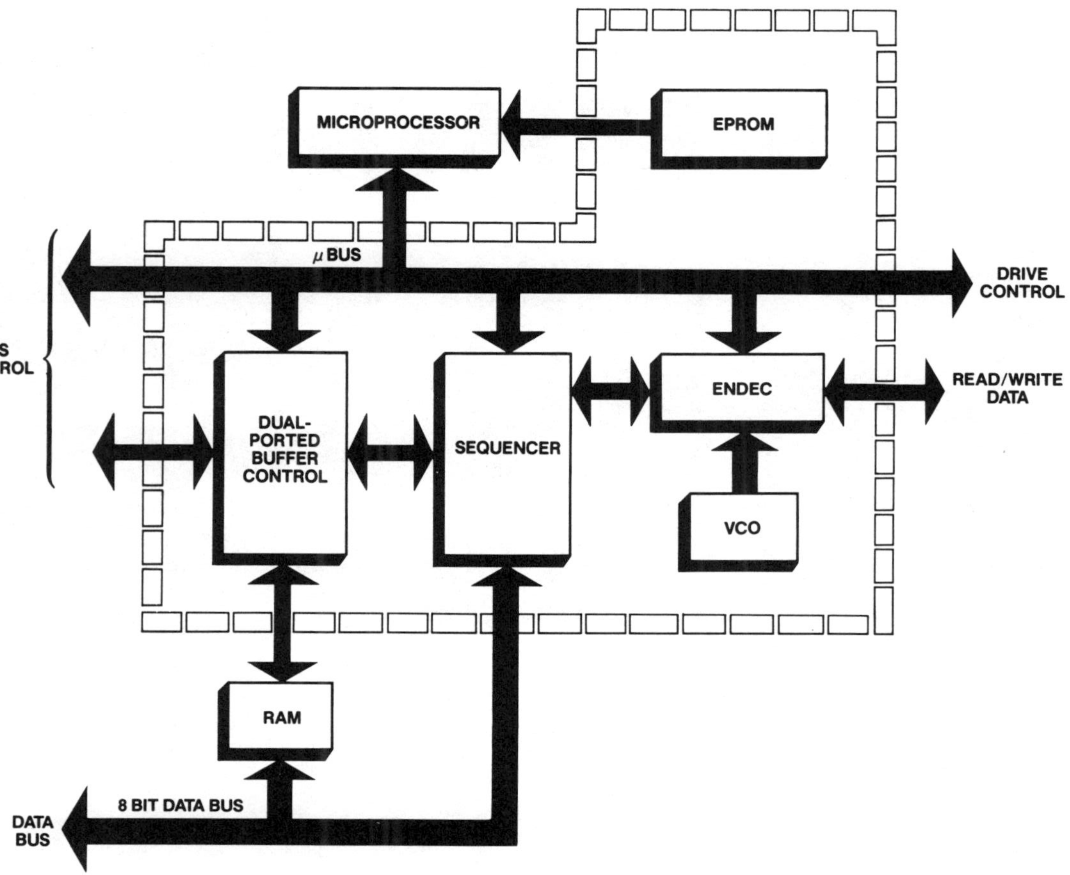

FIGURE 8–4
The SASI/SCSI interface defines a local bus for disk I/O.

Courtesy of Adaptec.

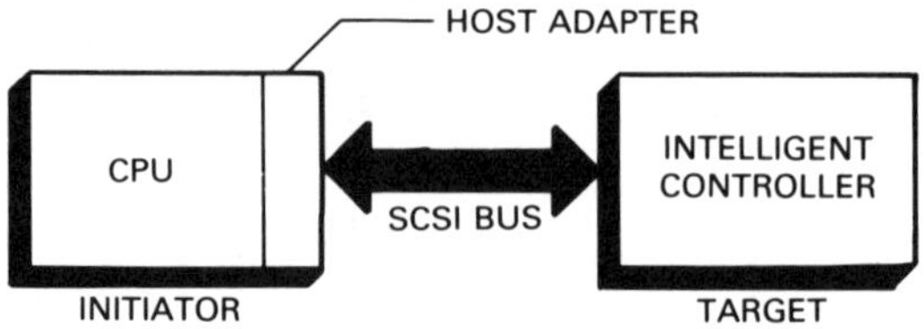

FIGURE 8–5
Two devices on the SCSI bus can communicate at one time.

computer and software can stay constant. The same software driver works for all drives. You and your customers won't be left out in the cold.

The SCSI bus supports some fairly complex configurations. If you start with a simple system—one computer and one disk drive—the relationship is obvious. But how do you control more complex combinations? The bus is restricted to communication between two devices at a time. The device that requires access (usually the host computer) becomes the *initiator* device. The disk drive becomes the *target* device, as shown in Figure 8–5.

In a complex system, therefore, all you have to do is maintain this relationship. No matter how many devices are

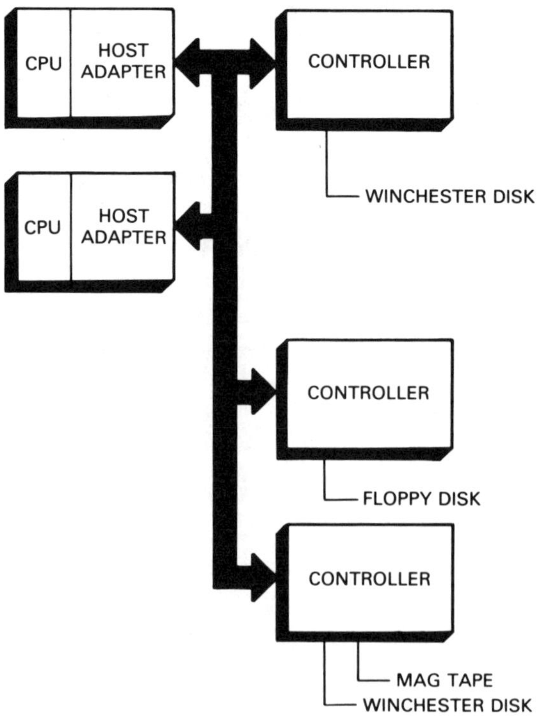

FIGURE 8–6
You can construct reasonably complex systems using the SCSI bus.

present on the bus, only two, one initiator and one target, can be in communication at any one time.

This isn't too difficult to enforce because each SCSI device must conform to the message protocol of the SCSI standard. Thus, each computer has a host adapter, and each (logical) peripheral will have its own controller, as shown in Figure 8–6, that implements the standard.

You can mix and match CPUs and intelligent controllers on the bus as much as you please, but the SCSI specification limits you to eight logical devices total. That gives you a great deal of opportunity for designing a flexible computer system with effective mass storage.

WHERE TO BEGIN

You've been exposed to a great deal of information now, and the only thing to do is to start using it. Get a copy of the SCSI specification. We've only scratched the surface of this detailed document. After you've read it, take a look at how hard it might be to design a system that has the SCSI standard in mind. That's a good way to learn something about its virtues and limitations.

In writing it is said that if you use a word 10 times, it is yours. A similar adage applies to electronics: Hands-on design teaches more than books. Good luck.

Epilogue

The exciting thing about writing on subjects in the realm of high technology is that they are always in flux, ever changing. What is new and innovative as this book is written, however, could easily become old news as the book is being edited and printed. This is the cutting edge. There's no escaping such a problem. We can only dodge it. I have attempted, to some extent, to avoid it by concentrating on basic principles rather than trends. Yet, it isn't clear to me that escape is necessary. Perhaps even the disappearance of a technological alternative will lend some perspective to the next generation of attempts. Edison is quoted as saying, "Now we know thousands of things that don't work." Failure teaches. Most of us would hesitate to build an aircraft modeled on the dodo bird.

Experience teaches that even a book on design cannot please everyone. There will be firms who are hurt because their products are not mentioned between its covers. There will be firms with products of limited appeal, whose value lies outside the scope of this book.

But this book isn't an exhaustive research book on the history of disk drives. It is a designer's guide. And I hope you find it a good guide. Still, I won't be surprised to hear that your successes come not so much along the main thoroughfares we've mapped out as on uncharted side roads. Technology is like that. Success is like that. And serendipity plays a vital role in an engineer's daily work.

References

The following books and articles served as references for this book and may offer additional information that will clarify it all for you.

Adams, Arlon T., *Electromagnetics for Engineers,* Roland Press Company, New York, 1971.

Booth, Grace M., *The Design of Complex Information Systems,* McGraw-Hill Inc., New York, 1983.

Glover, Neal, *Practical Error Correction Design for Engineers,* Data Systems Technology, Broomfield, Colorado, 1982. Call (303) 466-5228.

Kadison, Eric M., "5¼-in. floppy disk format looks to spread software," *Electronic Design,* December 23, 1982, p. 135.

Massey, William, *A Two-seven Designer's Guide for Digital Magnetic Recording,* William Massey, 1982. Call (303) 466-5923.

Matrick, Richard E., *Computer Storage Systems and Technology,* John Wiley & Sons, New York, 1977.

SCSI Buyer's Guide, Adaptive Data & Energy Systems, November, 1982, Issue 1. Write to 2627 Pomona Blvd, Pomona, California 91768.

Streaming, Archive Corp., 3540 Cadillac Ave., Costa Mesa, California, 92626. ISBN 0-9608810-0-X.

Trifari, John, "Computer Disks: Capacity Soars, Costs Plummet," *High Technology,* January 1983, p. 47.

Warren, Carl, "Partial 8-in. disc-drive standard lets most manufacturers forge ahead," *EDN,* May 5, 1980, p. 51.

Young, John F., *Cybernetic Engineering,* Halstead Press, New York, 1973.

Index